Bass

Adirondack Museum

5/25/08

W9-ADX-137

WOODCRAFT
AND CAMPING
by
"Nessmuk"

DOVER PUBLICATIONS, INC.

NEW YORK

This Dover edition, first published in 1963, is a slightly abridged and edited republication of the work published by Forest and Stream Publishing Company, New York, in 1920 under the title *Woodcraft*.

International Standard Book Number: 0-486-21145-2
Library of Congress Catalog Card Number: 63-21680

Manufactured in the United States of America
Dover Publications, Inc.
31 East 2nd Street, Mineola, N.Y. 11501

Preface

Woodcraft is dedicated to the Grand Army of "Outers," as a pocket volume of reference on—woodcraft.

> For brick and mortar breed filth and crime,
> With a pulse of evil that throbs and beats;
> And men are withered before their prime
> By the curse paved in with the lanes and streets.
>
> And lungs are poisoned and shoulders bowed,
> In the smothering reek of mill and mine;
> And death stalks in on the struggling crowd—
> But he shuns the shadow of oak and pine.

NESSMUK.

Contents

Illustrations

Chapter I

OVERWORK AND RECREATION—OUTING AND OUTERS
HOW TO DO IT, AND WHY THEY MISS IT

T DOES not need that Herbert Spencer should cross the ocean to tell us that we are an overworked nation; that our hair turns gray ten years earlier than the Englishman's; or, "that we have had somewhat too much of the gospel of work," and, "it is time to preach the gospel of relaxation." It is all true. But we work harder, accomplish more in a given time, and last quite as long as slower races. As to the gray hair—perhaps gray hair is better than none; and it is a fact that the average Briton becomes bald as early as the American turns gray. There is, however, a sad significance in his words when he says: "In every circle I have met men who had themselves suffered from nervous collapse due to stress of business, or named friends who had either killed themselves by overwork, or had been permanently incapacitated, or had wasted long periods in endeavors to recover health." Too true. And it is the constant strain, without let-up or relaxation, that, in nine cases out of ten, snaps the cord and ends in what the doctors call "nervous prostration"—something akin to paralysis—from which the sufferer seldom wholly recovers.

Mr. Spencer quotes that quaint old chronicler, Froissart, as saying, "The English take their pleasures sadly, after their fashion"; and thinks if he lived now, he would say of Americans, "they take their pleasures hurriedly, after their fashion." Perhaps.

It is an age of hurry and worry. Anything slower than steam is apt to "get left." Fortunes are quickly made and freely spent.

Nearly all busy, hard-worked Americans have an intuitive sense of the need that exists for at least one period of rest and relaxation during each year, and all—or nearly all—are willing to pay liberally, too liberally in fact, for anything that conduces to rest, recreation and sport. I am sorry to say that we mostly get swindled. As an average, the summer outer who goes to forest, lake or stream for health and sport, gets about ten cents' worth for a dollar of outlay. A majority will admit—to themselves at least—that after a month's vacation, they return to work with an inward consciousness of being somewhat disappointed—and beaten. We are free with our money when we have it. We are known throughout the civilized world for our lavishness in paying for our pleasures; but it humiliates us to know we have been beaten, and this is what the most of us know at the end of a summer vacation. To the man of millions it makes little difference. He is able to pay liberally for boats, buckboards and "body service," if he chooses to spend a summer in the North Woods. He has no need to study the questions of lightness and economy in a forest and stream outing. Let his guides take care of him; and unto them and the landlords he will give freely of his substance.

I do not write for him, and can do him little good. But there are hundreds of thousands of practical, useful men, many of them far from being rich; mechanics, artists, writers, merchants, clerks, business men—workers, so to speak—who sorely need and well deserve a season of rest and relaxation at least once a year. To these, and for these, I write.

Perhaps more than fifty years of devotion to "woodcraft" may enable me to give a few useful hints and suggestions to those whose dreams, during the close season of work, are of camp-life by flood, field and forest.

I have found that nearly all who have a real love of nature and out-of-door camp-life, spend a good deal of time and talk in planning future trips, or discussing the trips and pleasures gone by, but still dear to memory.

When the mountain streams are frozen and the Nor'land winds are out;

when the winter winds are drifting the bitter sleet and snow; when winter rains are making out-of-door life unendurable;

when season, weather and law combine to make it "close time" for beast, bird and man, it is well that a few congenial spirits should, at some favorite trysting place, gather around the glowing stove and exchange yarns, opinions and experiences. Perhaps no two will exactly agree on the best ground for an outing, on the flies, rods, reels, guns, etc., or half a dozen other points that may be discussed. But one thing all admit. Each and every one has gone to his chosen ground with too much impedimenta, too much duffle; and nearly all have used boats at least twice as heavy as they need to have been. The temptation to buy this or that bit of indispensable camp-kit has been too strong, and we have gone to the blessed woods, handicapped with a load fit for a pack-mule. This is not how to do it.

Go light; the lighter the better, so that you have the simplest material for health, comfort and enjoyment.

Of course, if you intend to have a permanent camp, and can reach it by boat or wagon, lightness is not so important, though even in that case it is well to guard against taking a lot of stuff that is likely to prove of more weight than worth—only to leave it behind when you come out.

As to clothing for the woods, a good deal of nonsense has been written about "strong, coarse woolen clothes." You do not want coarse woolen clothes. Fine woolen cassimere of medium thickness for coat, vest and pantaloons, with no cotton lining. Color, slate gray or dead-leaf (either is good). Two soft, thick woolen shirts; two pairs of fine, but substantial, woolen drawers; two pairs of strong woolen socks or stockings; these are what you need, and all you need in the way of clothing for the woods, excepting hat and boots, or gaiters. Boots are best—providing you do not let yourself be inveigled into wearing a pair of long-legged heavy boots with thick soles, as has been often advised by writers who knew no better. Heavy, long-legged boots are a weary, tiresome incumbrance on a hard tramp through rough woods. Even moccasins are better. Gaiters, all sorts of high shoes, in fact, are too bothersome about fastening and unfastening. Light boots are best. Not thin, unserviceable affairs, but light as to actual weight. The following hints will give an idea for the best footgear for the woods; let them be single soled, single backs and single fronts, except light, short foot-linings. Back of solid "country kip"; fronts of substan-

tial French calf; heel one inch high, with steel nails; countered
outside; straps narrow, of fine French calf put on "astraddle,"
and set down to the top of the back. The out-sole stout,
Spanish oak, and pegged rather than sewed, although either is
good. They will weigh considerably less than half as much as
the clumsy, costly boots usually recommended for the woods;
and the added comfort must be tested to be understood.

The hat should be fine, soft felt with moderately low crown
and wide brim; color to match the clothing.

The proper covering for head and feet is no slight affair,
and will be found worth some attention. Be careful that the
boots are not too tight, or the hat too loose. The above rig
will give the tourist one shirt, one pair of drawers and a pair
of socks to carry as extra clothing. A soft, warm blanket-bag,
open at the ends, and just long enough to cover the sleeper,
with an oblong square of waterproofed cotton cloth 6x8 feet,
will give warmth and shelter by night and will weigh together
five or six pounds. This, with the extra clothing, will make
about eight pounds of dry goods to pack over carries, which
is enough. Probably, also, it will be found little enough for
comfort.

During a canoe cruise across the Northern Wilderness in
the late summer, I met many parties at different points in the
woods, and the amount of unnecessary duffle with which they
encumbered themselves was simply appalling. Why a shrewd
business man, who goes through with a guide and makes a forest hotel his camping ground nearly every night, should handi-
cap himself with a five-peck pack basket full of gray woolen
and gum blankets, extra clothing, pots, pans, and kettles, with
a 9-pound 10-bore, and two rods—yes, and an extra pair of
heavy boots hanging astride of the gun—well, it is one of the
things I shall never understand. My own load, including canoe,
extra clothing, blanket-bag, two days' rations, pocket-axe, rod
and knapsack, never exceeded 26 pounds; and I went prepared
to camp out any and every night.

People who contemplate an outing in the woods are pretty
apt to commence preparations a long way ahead, and to pick
up many trifling articles that suggest themselves as useful and
handy in camp; all well enough in their way, but making at

least a too heavy load. It is better to commence by studying
to ascertain just how light one can go through without especial discomfort. A good plan is to think over the trip during
leisure hours, and make out a list of indispensable articles, se-
curing them beforehand, and have them stowed in handy fashion, so that nothing needful may be missing just when and
where it cannot be procured. The list will be longer than one
would think, but need not be cumbersome or heavy. As I am
usually credited with making a cruise or a long woods tramp
with exceptionally light duffle, I will give a list of the articles
I take along—going on foot over carries or through the woods.

Chapter II

KNAPSACK, HATCHET, KNIVES, TINWARE, RODS, FISHING TACKLE, DITTY-BAG

T HE clothing, blanket-bag and shelter-cloth are all that need be described in that line. The next articles that I look after are knapsack (or pack basket), rod with reel, lines, flies, hooks, and all my fishing gear, pocket-axe, knives and tinware. Firstly, the knapsack; as you are apt to carry it a great many miles, it is well to have it right, and easy-fitting at the start. Don't be induced to carry a pack basket. I am aware that it is in high favor all through the Northern Wilderness, and is also much used in other localities where guides and sportsmen most do congregate. But I do not like it. I admit that it will carry a loaf of bread, with tea, sugar, etc., without jamming; that bottles, crockery, and other fragile duffle is safer from breakage than in an oil-cloth knapsack. But it is by no means waterproof in a rain or a splashing head sea, is more than twice as heavy—always growing heavier as it gets wetter—and I had rather have bread, tea, sugar, etc., a little jammed than water-soaked. Also, it may be remarked that man is a vertebrate animal and ought to respect his backbone. The loaded pack basket on a heavy carry never fails to get in on the most vulnerable knob of the human vertebrae. The knapsack sits easy, and does not chafe. The one shown in the engraving is of good form; and the original—which I have carried for years—is satisfactory in every respect. It holds over half a bushel, carries blanket-bag, shelter tent, hatchet, ditty-bag, tinware, fishing tackle, clothes and two days' rations. It weighs, empty, just twelve ounces.

KNAPSACK AND DITTY-BAG

The hatchet and knives shown in the engraving will be found to fill the bill satisfactorily so far as cutlery may be required. Each is good and useful of its kind, the hatchet especially, being the best model I have ever found for a "double-barreled" pocket-axe. And just here let me digress for a little chat on the indispensable hatchet; for it is the most difficult piece of camp kit to obtain in perfection of which I have any knowledge. Before I was a dozen years old I came to realize that a light hatchet was a sine qua non in woodcraft, and I also found it a most difficult thing to get. I tried shingling hatchets, lathing hatchets, and the small hatchets to be found in country hardware stores, but none of them were satisfactory. I had quite a number made by blacksmiths who professed skill in making edge tools, and these were the worst of all, being like nothing on the earth or under it—murderous-looking, clumsy, and all too heavy, with no balance or proportion. I had hunted twelve years before I caught up with the pocket-axe I was looking for. It was made in Rochester, by a surgical instrument maker named Bushnell. It cost time and money to get it. I worked one rainy Saturday fashioning the pattern in wood. Spoiled a day going to Rochester, waited a day for the blade, paid

HATCHET AND KNIVES

$3.00 for it, and lost a day coming home. Boat fare $1.00, and expenses $2.00, besides three days lost time, with another rainy Sunday for making leather sheath and hickory handle.

My witty friends, always willing to help me out in figuring the cost of my hunting and fishing gear, made the following business-like estimate, which they placed where I would be certain to see it the first thing in the morning. Premising that of the five who assisted in that little joke, all stronger, bigger fellows than myself, four have gone "where they never see the sun," I will copy the statement as it stands today, on paper yellow with age. For I have kept it over forty years.

A WOODSMAN,

Dr.

To getting up one limber-go-shiftless pocket-axe:

Cost of blade	$3 00
Fare on boat	1 00
Expenses for 3 days	3 00
Three days lost time at $1.25 per day	3 75
Two days making model, handle and sheath, say	2 00
Total	$12 75
Per contra, by actual value of axe	2 00
Balance	$10 75

Then they raised a horse laugh, and the cost of that hatchet became a standing joke and a slur on my "business ability." What aggravated me most was, that the rascals were not so far out in their calculation. And was I so far wrong? That hatchet was my favorite for nearly thirty years. It has been "upset" twice by skilled workmen; and, if my friend "Bero" has not lost it, is still in service.

Would I have gone without it any year for one or two dollars? But I prefer the double blade. I want one thick, stunt edge for knots, deers' bones, etc., and a fine, keen edge for cutting clear timber.

A word as to knife, or knives. These are of prime necessity, and should be of the best, both as to shape and temper. The "bowies" and "hunting knives" usually kept on sale, are thick, clumsy affairs, with a sort of ridge along the middle of the blade, murderous-looking, but of little use; rather fitted to adorn a dime novel or the belt of "Billy the Kid," than the outfit of the hunter. The one shown in the cut is thin in the blade, and handy for skinning, cutting meat, or eating with. The strong double-bladed pocket knife is the best model I have yet found, and, in connection with the sheath knife, is all sufficient for camp use. It is not necessary to take table cutlery into the woods. A good fork may be improvised from a beech or birch stick; and the half of a fresh-water mussel shell, with a split stick by way of handle, makes an excellent spoon.

My entire outfit for cooking and eating dishes comprises five pieces of tinware. This is when stopping in a permanent camp. When cruising and tramping, I take just two pieces in the knapsack.

I get a skillful tinsmith to make one dish as follows: Six inches on bottom, 6¾ inches on top, side 2 inches high. The bottom is of the heaviest tin procurable, the sides of lighter tin, and seamed to be water-tight without solder. The top simply turned, without wire. The second dish to be made the same, but small enough to nest in the first, and also to fit into it when inverted as a cover. Two other dishes made from common pressed tinware, with the tops cut off and turned, also without wire. They are fitted so that they all nest, taking no more room than the largest dish alone, and each of the three smaller dishes makes a perfect cover for the next larger. The other piece is a tin camp-kettle, also of the heaviest tin, and seamed water-tight. It holds two quarts, and the other dishes nest in it perfectly, so that when packed the whole takes just as much room as the kettle alone. I should mention that the strong ears are set below the rim of the kettle, and the bale falls outside, so, as none of the dishes have any handle, there are no aggravating "stickouts" to wear and abrade. The snug affair weighs, all told, two pounds. I have met parties in the North Woods whose one frying pan weighed more—with its handle three feet long. How ever did they get through the brush with such a culinary terror?

It is only when I go into a very accessible camp that I take so much as five pieces of tinware along. I once made a ten days' tramp through an unbroken wilderness on foot, and all the dish I took was a ten-cent tin; it was enough. I believe I will tell the story of that tramp before I get through. For I saw more game in the ten days than I ever saw before or since in a season; and I am told that the whole region is now a thrifty farming country, with the deer nearly all gone. They were plenty enough thirty-nine years ago this very month.

I feel more diffidence in speaking of rods than of any other matter connected with out-door sports. The number and variety of rods and makers; the enthusiasm of trout and fly "cranks"; the fact that angling does not take precedence of all other sports with me, with the humiliating confession that I am not above bucktail spinners, worms and sinkers, minnow tails and white grubs—this and these constrain me to be brief.

But, as I have been a fisher all my life, from my pinhook days to the present time; as I have run the list pretty well up, from brook minnows to 100-pound albacores, I may be pardoned for a few remarks on the rod and the use thereof.

A rod may be a very high-toned, high-priced aesthetic plaything, costing $50 to $75, or it may be—a rod. A serviceable and splendidly balanced rod can be obtained from first class makers for less money. By all means let the man of money indulge his fancy for the most costly rod that can be procured. He might do worse. A practical every day sportsman whose income is limited will find that a more modest product will drop his flies on the water quite as attractively to *Salmo fontinalis*. My little 8½-foot, 4¾-ounce split bamboo which the editor of *Forest and Stream* had made for me cost $10.00. I have given it hard usage and at times large trout have tested it severely, but it has never failed me. The dimensions of my second rod are 9½ feet long and 5¾ ounces in weight. This rod will handle the bucktail spinners which I use for trout and bass, when other things have failed. I used a rod of this description for several summers both in Adirondack and western waters. It had a hand-made reel seat, agate first guide, was satisfactory in every respect, and I could see in balance, action, and appearance no superiority in a rod costing $25.00, which one of my friends sported. Charles Dudley Warner, who writes charmingly of woods life, has the following in regard to trout fishing, which is so neatly humorous that it will bear repeating:

"It is well known that no person who regards his reputation will ever kill a trout with anything but a fly. It requires some training on the part of the trout to take to this method. The uncultivated trout in unfrequented waters prefers the bait; and the rural people, whose sole object in going a-fishing appears to be to catch fish, indulge them in their primitive state for the worm. No sportsman, however, will use anything but a fly —except he happens to be alone." Speaking of rods, he says: "The rod is a bamboo weighing seven ounces, which has to be spliced with a winding of silk thread every time it is used. This is a tedious process; but, by fastening the joints in this way, a uniform spring is secured in the rod. No one devoted to high art would think of using a socket joint."

One summer during a seven weeks' tour in the Northern Wilderness, my only rod was a 7½ foot Henshall. It came to hand with two bait-tips only; but I added a fly-tip, and it made an excellent "general fishing rod." With it I could handle a large bass or pickerel; it was a capital bait-rod for brook trout; as fly rod it has pleased me well enough. It is likely to go with me again. For reel casting, the 5½ foot rod is handier. But it is not yet decided which is best, and I leave every man his own opinion. Only, I think one rod enough, but have always had more.

And don't neglect to take what sailors call a "ditty-bag."

This may be a little sack of chamois leather about 4 inches wide by 6 inches in length. Mine is before me as I write. Emptying the contents, I find it inventories as follows: A dozen hooks, running in size from small minnow hooks to large Limericks; four lines of six yards each, varying from the finest to a size sufficient for a ten-pound fish; three darning needles and a few common sewing needles; a dozen buttons; sewing silk; thread, and a small ball of strong yarn for darning socks; sticking salve; a bit of shoemaker's wax; beeswax; sinkers, and a very fine file for sharpening hooks. The ditty-bag weighs, with contents, 2½ ounces; and it goes in a small buckskin bullet pouch, which I wear almost as constantly as my hat. The pouch has a sheath strongly sewed on the back side of it, where the light hunting knife is always at hand, and it also carries a two-ounce vial of fly medicine, a vial of "pain killer," and two or three gangs of hooks on brass wire snells—of which, more in another place. I can always go down into that pouch for a water-proof match safe, strings, compass, bits of linen and scarlet flannel (for frogging), copper tacks, and other light duffle. It is about as handy a piece of woods-kit as I carry.

I hope no aesthetic devotee of the fly-rod will lay down the book in disgust when I confess to a weakness for frogging. I admit that it is not high-toned sport; and yet I have got a good deal of amusement out of it. The persistence with which a large batrachian will snap at a bit of red flannel after being several times hooked on the same lure, and the comical way in which he will scuttle off with a quick succession of short jumps after each release; the cheerful manner in which, after each bout, he will tune up his deep, bass pipe—ready for another greedy snap at an ibis fly or red rag—is rather funny. And his hind legs, rolled in meal and nicely browned, are preferable to trout or venison.

Chapter III

GETTING LOST—CAMPING OUT—ROUGHING IT OR
SMOOTHING IT—INSECTS—CAMPS, AND HOW TO
MAKE THEM

 ITH a large majority of prospective tourists and outers, "camping out" is a leading factor in the summer vacation. And during the long winter months they are prone to collect in little knots and talk much of camps, fishing, hunting, and "roughing it." The last phrase is very popular and always cropping out in the talks on matters pertaining to a vacation in the woods. I dislike the phrase. We do not go to the green woods and crystal waters to rough it, we go to smooth it. We get it rough enough at home; in towns and cities; in shops, offices, stores, banks—anywhere that we may be placed—with the necessity always present of being on time and up to our work; of providing for the dependent ones; of keeping up, catching up, or getting left. "Alas for the life-long battle, whose bravest slogan is bread."

As for the few fortunate ones who have no call to take a hand in any strife or struggle, who not only have all the time there is, but a great deal that they cannot dispose of with any satisfaction to themselves or anybody else—I am not writing for them; but only to those of the world's workers who go, or would like to go, every summer to the woods. And to these I would say, don't rough it; make it as smooth, as restful and pleasurable as you can.

To this end you need pleasant days and peaceful nights. You cannot afford to be tormented and poisoned by insects, nor kept awake at night by cold and damp, nor to exhaust your strength by hard tramps and heavy loads. Take it easy, and always keep cool. Nine men out of ten, on finding themselves lost in the woods, fly into a panic, and quarrel with the compass. Never do that. The compass is always right, or nearly so. It is not many years since an able-bodied man—sportsman of course—lost his way in the North Woods, and took fright, as might be expected. He was well armed and well found for a week in the woods. What ought to have been only an interesting adventure, became a tragedy. He tore through thickets and swamps in his senseless panic, until he dropped and died through fright, hunger and exhaustion.

A well authenticated story is told of a guide in the Oswegatchie region, who perished in the same way. Guides are not infallible; I have known more than one to get lost. Wherefore, should you be tramping through a pathless forest on a cloudy day, and should the sun suddenly break from under a cloud in the northwest about noon, don't be scared. The last day is not at hand, and the planets have not become mixed; only, you are turned. You have gradually swung around, until you are facing northwest when you meant to travel south. It has a muddling effect on the mind—this getting lost in the woods. But, if you can collect and arrange your gray brain matter, and suppress all panicky feeling, it is easily got along with. For instance; it is morally certain that you commenced swinging to southwest, then west, to northwest. Had you kept on until you were heading directly north, you could rectify your course simply by following a true south course. But, as you have varied three-eighths of the circle, set your compass and travel by it to the southeast, until, in your judgment, you have about made up the deviation; then go straight south, and you will not be far wrong. Carry the compass in your hand and look at it every few minutes; for the tendency to swerve from a straight course when a man is once lost—and nearly always to the right—is a thing past understanding.

As regards poisonous insects, it may be said that, to the man with clean, bleached, tender skin, they are, at the start, an unendurable torment. No one can enjoy life with a smarting, burning, swollen face, while the attacks on every exposed inch of skin are persistent and constant. I have seen a young man after two days' exposure to these pests come out of the woods with one eye entirely closed and the brow hanging over it like a clam shell, while face and hands were almost hideous from inflammation and puffiness. The St. Regis and St. Francis Indians, although born and reared in the woods, by no means make light of the black fly.

It took the man who could shoot Phantom Falls to find out, "Its bite is not severe, nor is it ordinarily poisonous. There may be an occasional exception to this rule; but beside the bite of the mosquito, it is comparatively mild and harmless." And again: "Gnats . . . in my way of thinking, are much worse than the black fly or mosquito." So says Murray. Our observations differ. A thousand mosquitoes and as many gnats can bite me without leaving a mark, or having any effect save the pain of the bite while they are at work. But each bite of the black fly makes a separate and distinct boil, that will not heal and be well in two months.

While fishing for brook trout in July last, I ran into a swarm of them on Moose River, and got badly bitten. I had carelessly left my medicine behind. On the first of October the bites had not ceased to be painful, and it was three months before they disappeared entirely. Frank Forester says, in his *Fish and Fishing,* page 371, that he has never fished for the red-fleshed trout of Hamilton county, "being deterred therefrom by dread of that curse of the summer angler, the black fly, which is to me especially venomous."

"Adirondack Murray" gives extended directions for beating these little pests by the use of buckskin gloves with chamois gauntlets, Swiss mull, fine muslin, etc. Then he advises a mixture of sweet oil and tar, which is to be applied to face and hands; and he adds that it is easily washed off, leaving the skin soft and smooth as an infant's; all of which is true. But, more than forty years' experience in the woods has taught me that the following recipe is infallible anywhere that *sancudos, moquims,* or our own poisonous insects do most abound.

It was published in *Forest and Stream* in the summer of 1880, and again in '83. It has been pretty widely quoted and adopted, and I have never known it to fail: Three ounces pine tar, two ounces castor oil, one ounce pennyroyal oil. Simmer all together over a slow fire, and bottle for use. You will hardly need more than a two-ounce vial full in a season. One ounce has lasted me six weeks in the woods. Rub it in thoroughly and liberally at first, and after you have established a good glaze, a little replenishing from day to day will be sufficient. And don't fool with soap and towels where insects are plenty. A good safe coat of this varnish grows better the longer it is kept on—and it is cleanly and wholesome. If you get your face and hands crocky or smutty about the camp-fire, wet the corner of your handkerchief and rub it off, not forgetting to apply the varnish at once, wherever you have cleaned it off. Last summer I carried a cake of soap and a towel in my knapsack through the North Woods for a seven weeks' tour, and never used either a single time. When I had established a good glaze on the skin, it was too valuable to be sacrificed for any weak whim connected with soap and water. When I struck a woodland hotel, I found soap and towels plenty enough. I found the mixture gave one's face the ruddy tanned look supposed to be indicative of health and hard muscle. A thorough ablution in the public wash basin reduced the color, but left the skin very soft and smooth; in fact, as a lotion for the skin it is excellent. It is a soothing and healing application for poisonous bites already received.

I have given some space to the insect question, but no more than it deserves or requires. The venomous little wretches are quite important enough to spoil many a well planned trip to the woods, and it is best to beat them from the start. You will find that immunity from insects and a comfortable camp are the two first and most indispensable requisites of an outing in the woods. And just here I will briefly tell how a young friend of mine went to the woods, some twenty-five years ago. He was a bank clerk, and a good fellow withal, with a leaning toward camp-life.

For months, whenever we met, he would introduce his favorite topics, fishing, camping out, etc. At last in the hottest of the hot months, the time came. He put in an appearance with a fighting cut on his hair, a little stiff straw hat, and a soft skin, bleached by long confinement in a close office. I thought he looked a little tender; but he was sanguine. He could rough it, could sleep on the bare ground with the root of a tree for a pillow; as for mosquitoes and punkies, he never minded them.

We went in a party of five—two old hunters and three youngsters, the latter all enthusiasm and pluck—at first. Toward the last end of a heavy eight-mile tramp, they grew silent, and slapped and scratched nervously. Arriving at the camping spot, they worked fairly well, but were evidently weakening a little. By the time we were ready to turn in they were reduced pretty well to silence and suffering—especially the bank clerk, Jean L. The punkies were eager for his tender skin, and they were rank poison to him. He muffled his head in a blanket and tried to sleep, but it was only a partial success. When, by suffocating himself, he obtained a little relief from insect bites, there were stubs and knotty roots continually poking themselves among his ribs, or digging into his backbone.

I have often had occasion to observe that stubs, roots and small stones, etc., have a perverse tendency to abrade the anatomy of people unused to the woods. Mr. C. D. Warner has noticed the same thing, I believe.

On the whole, Jean and the other youngsters behaved very well. Although they turned out in the morning with red, swollen faces and half closed eyes, they all went trouting and caught about 150 small trout between them. They did their level bravest to make a jolly thing of it; but Jean's attempt to watch a deerlick, resulted in a wetting through the sudden advent of a shower; and the shower drove about all the punkies and mosquitoes in the neighborhood under our roof for shelter. I never saw them more plentiful or worse. Jean gave in and varnished his pelt thoroughly with my "punkie dope," as he called it; but, too late; the mischief was done. And the second trial was worse to those youngsters than the first. More insects. More stubs and knots. Owing to these little annoyances, they arrived at home several days before their friends expected them—leaving enough rations in camp to last Old Sile and the writer a full week. And the moral of it is, if they had fitted themselves for the the woods before going there, the trip would have been a pleasure instead of a misery.

One other little annoyance I will mention, as a common oc-
currence among those who camp out; this is the lack of a pillow. I suppose I have camped fifty times with people, who, on
turning in, were squirming around for a long time, trying to
get a rest for the head. Boots are the most common resort. But,
when you place a boot-leg—or two of them—under your head,
they collapse, and make a head-rest less than half an inch thick.
Just why it never occurs to people that a stuffing of moss, leaves,
or hemlock browse, would fill out the bootleg and make a passable pillow, is another conundrum I cannot answer. But there
is another and better way of making a pillow for camp use,
which I will describe further on.

And now I wish to devote some space to one of the most important adjuncts of woodcraft, i.e., camps; how to make them,
and how to make them comfortable. There are camps, and
camps. There are camps in the North Woods that are really
fine villas, costing thousands of dollars, and there are log-
houses, and shanties, and bark camps, and A tents, and walled
tents, shelter tents and shanty tents. But, I assume that the
camp best fitted to the wants of the average outer is the one
that combines the essentials of dryness, lightness, portability,
cheapness, and is easily and quickly put up. Another essential
is, that it must admit of a bright fire in front by night or day.
I will give short descriptions of the forest shelters (camps) I
have found handiest and most useful.

Firstly, I will mention a sort of camp that was described in a
sportsman's paper, and has since been largely quoted and used.
It is made by fastening a horizontal pole to a couple of contigu-
ous trees, and then putting on a heavy covering of hemlock
boughs, shingling them with the tips downward, of course. A
fire is to be made at the roots of one of the trees. This, with
plenty of boughs, may be made to stand a pretty stiff rain; but
it is only a damp arbor, and no camp, properly speaking. A
forest camp should always admit of a bright fire in front, with
a lean-to or shed roof overhead, to reflect the fire heat on the
bedding below. Any camp that falls short of this, lacks the requirements of warmth, brightness and healthfulness. This is
why I discard all close, canvas tents.

The simplest and most primitive of all camps is the "Indian

camp." It is easily and quickly made, is warm and comfortable, and stands a pretty heavy rain when properly put up. This is how it is made: Let us say you are out and have slightly missed your way. The coming gloom warns you that night is shutting down. You are no tenderfoot. You know that a place of rest is essential to health and comfort through the long, cold November night. You dive down the first little hollow until you strike a rill of water, for water is a prime necessity. As you draw your hatchet you take in the whole situation at a glance. The little stream is gurgling downward in a half choked frozen way. There is a huge sodden hemlock lying across it. One clip of the hatchet shows it will peel. There is plenty of smaller timber standing around; long, slim poles, with a tuft of foliage on

INDIAN CAMP

top. Five minutes suffice to drop one of these, cut a twelve-foot pole from it, sharpen the pole at each end, jam one end into the ground and the other into the rough back of a scraggy hemlock, and there is your ridge pole. Now go—with your hatchet— for the bushiest and most promising young hemlocks within reach. Drop them and draw them to camp rapidly. Next, you need a fire. There are fifty hard, resinous limbs sticking up from the prone hemlock; lop off a few of these, and split the largest into match timber; reduce the splinters to shavings, scrape the wet leaves from your prospective fireplace, and strike a match on the balloon part of your trousers. If you are a woodsman you will strike but one. Feed the fire slowly at first; it will gain fast. When you have a blaze ten feet high, look at your watch. It is 6 P. M. You don't want to turn in before 10 o'clock, and you have four hours to kill before bed-time. Now, tackle the old hemlock; take off every dry limb, and then peel the bark and bring it to camp. You will find this takes an hour or more.

Next, strip every limb from your young hemlocks, and shingle them onto your ridge pole. This will make a sort of bear den, very well calculated to give you a comfortable night's rest. The bright fire will soon dry the ground that is to be your bed, and you will have plenty of time to drop another small hemlock and make a bed of browse a foot thick. You do it. Then you make your pillow. Now, this pillow is essential to comfort and very simple. It is half a yard of muslin, sewed up as a bag, and filled with moss or hemlock browse. You can empty it and put it in your pocket, where it takes up about as much room as a handkerchief. You have other little muslin bags—an' you be wise. One holds a couple of ounces of good tea; another, sugar; another is kept to put your loose duffle in: money, match safe, pocket-knife. You have a pat of butter and a bit of pork, with a liberal slice of brown bread; and before turning in you make a cup of tea, broil a slice of pork, and indulge in a lunch.

Ten o'clock comes. The time has not passed tediously. You are warm, dry and well-fed. Your old friends, the owls, come near the fire-light and salute you with their strange wild notes; a distant fox sets up for himself with his odd, barking cry and you turn in. Not ready to sleep just yet.

But you drop off; and it is two bells in the morning watch when you waken with a sense of chill and darkness. The fire has burned low, and snow is falling. The owls have left, and a deep silence broods over the cold, still forest. You rouse the fire, and, as the bright light shines to the furthest recesses of your forest den, get out the little pipe, and reduce a bit of navy plug to its lowest denomination. The smoke curls lazily upward; the fire makes you warm and drowsy, and again you lie down—to again awaken with a sense of chilliness—to find the fire burned low, and daylight breaking. You have slept better than you would in your own room at home. You have slept in an "Indian camp."

You have also learned the difference between such a simple shelter and an open air bivouac under a tree or beside an old log.

Another easily made and very comfortable camp is the "brush shanty," as it is usually called in Northern Pennsylvania. The frame for such a shanty is a cross-pole resting on two crotches about six feet high, and enough straight poles to make a foundation for the thatch. The poles are laid about six inches apart, one end of the ground, the other on the crosspole, and at a pretty sharp angle. The thatch is made of the fan-like boughs cut from the thrifty young hemlock, and are to be laid bottom upward and feather end down. Commence to lay them from the ground, and work up to the crosspole, shingling them carefully as you go. If the thatch be laid a foot in thickness, and well done, the shanty will stand a pretty heavy rain—better than the average bark roof, which is only rain-proof in dry weather.

A bark camp, however, may be a very neat sylvan affair, provided you are camping where spruce or balsam fir may be easily reached, and in the hot months when bark will "peel"; and you have a day in which to work at a camp. The best bark camps I have ever seen are in the Adirondacks. Some of them are rather elaborate in construction, requiring two or more days' hard labor by a couple of guides. When the stay is to be a long one, and the camp permanent, perhaps it will pay.

As good a camp as I have ever tried—perhaps the best—is the "shanty-tent," shown in the illustration. It is easily put up, is comfortable, neat, and absolutely rain-proof. Of course, it may be of any required size; but, for a party of two, the following dimensions and directions will be found all sufficient:

Firstly, the roof. This is merely a sheet of strong cotton cloth 9 feet long by 4 or 4½ feet in width. The sides, of the same material, to be 4½ feet deep at front, and 2 feet deep at the back. This gives 7 feet along the edge of the roof, leaving 2 feet for turning down at the back end of the shanty. It will be seen that the sides must be "cut bias," to compensate for the angle of the roof, otherwise the shanty will not be square and ship-shape when put up. Allowing for waste in cutting, it takes nearly 3 yards of cloth for each side. The only labor required in making, is to cut the sides to the proper shape, and stitch them to the roof. No buttons, strings, or loops. The cloth does not even require hemming. It does, however, need a little wa-ter-proofing; for which the following receipt will answer very well, and add little or nothing to the weight: To 10 quarts of water add 10 ounces of lime, and 4 ounces of alum; let it stand until clear; fold the cloth snugly and put it in another vessel, pour the solution on it, let it soak for 12 hours; then rinse in luke-warm rain water, stretch and dry in the sun, and the shanty-tent is ready for use.

To put it up properly, make a neat frame as follows: Two strong stakes or posts for the front, driven firmly in the ground 4½ feet apart; at a distance of 6 feet 10 inches from these, drive two other posts—these to be 4 feet apart—for back end of shanty. The front posts to be 4½ feet high, the back rests only two feet. The former also to incline a little toward each other above, so as to measure from outside of posts, just 4 feet at top. This gives a little more width at front end of shanty, adding space and warmth. No crotches are used in putting up the shanty-tent. Each of the four posts is fitted on the top to receive a flat-ended cross-pole, and admit of nailing. When the posts are squarely ranged and driven, select two straight, hard-wood rods, 2 inches in diameter, and 7 feet in length—or a little more. Flatten the ends carefully and truly, lay them alongside on top from post to post, and fasten them with a light nail at each end. Now, select two more straight rods of the same size, but a little over 4 feet in length; flatten the ends of these as you did the others, lay them crosswise from side to side, and lapping the ends of the other rods; fasten them solidly by driv-ing a sixpenny nail through the ends and into the posts, and you have a square frame 7x4 feet. But it is not yet complete. Three light rods are needed for rafters. These are to be placed lengthwise of the roof at equal distances apart, and nailed or tied to keep them in place. Then take two straight poles a lit-tle over 7 feet long, and some 3 inches in diameter. These are to be accurately flattened at the ends, and nailed to the bottom of the posts, snug to the ground, on outside of posts. A foot-log and head-log are indispensable. These should be about 5 inches in diameter, and of a length to just reach from outside to outside of posts. They should be squared at ends, and the foot-log placed against the front post, outside, and held firmly in place by two wooden pins. The head-log is fastened the same way, except that it goes against the inside of the back posts; and the frame is complete. Round off all sharp angles or corners with knife and hatchet, and proceed to spread and fasten the cloth. Lay the roof on evenly, and tack it truly to the front cross-rod, using about a dozen six-ounce tacks. Stretch the cloth to its bearings, and tack it at the back end in the same manner. Stretch it sidewise and tack the sides to the side poles, fore and aft. Tack front and back ends of sides to the front and back posts. Bring down the 2-foot flap of roof at back end of shanty; stretch, and tack it snugly to the back posts—and your sylvan house is done. It is rain-proof, wind-proof, warm and comfortable. The foot and head logs define the limits of your forest dwelling; within which you may pile fragrant hemlock browse as thick as you please, and renew it from day to day. It is the perfect camp.

You may put it up with less care and labor, and make it do very well. But I have tried to explain how to do it in the best manner; to make it all sufficient for an entire season. And it takes longer to tell it on paper than to do it.

When I go to the woods with a partner, and we arrive at our camping ground, I like him to get his fishing rig together, and start out for a half day's exercise with his favorite flies, leaving me to make the camp according to my own notions of wood-craft. If he will come back about dusk with a few pounds of trout, I will have a pleasant camp and a bright fire for him. And if he has enjoyed wading an icy stream more than I have making the camp—he has had a good day.

Perhaps it may not be out of place to say that the camp, made as above, calls for fifteen bits of timber, posts, rods, etc., a few shingle nails, and some six-penny wrought nails, with a paper of six-ounce tacks. Nails and tacks will weigh about five ounces, and are always useful. In tacking the cloth, turn the raw edge in until you have four thicknesses, as a single thickness is apt to tear. If you desire to strike camp, it takes about ten minutes to draw and save all the nails and tacks, fold the cloth smoothly, and deposit the whole in your knapsack. If you wish to get up a shelter tent on fifteen minutes' notice, cut and sharpen a twelve-foot pole as for the Indian camp, stick one end in the ground, the other in the rough bark of a large tree —hemlock is best—hang the cloth on the pole, fasten the sides to rods, and the rods to the ground with inverted crotches, and your shelter tent is ready for you to creep under.

The above description of the shanty-tent may seem a trifle elaborate, but I hope it is plain. The affair weighs just three pounds, and it takes a skillful woodsman about three hours of

SHANTY-TENT AND CAMP-FIRE

easy work to put it in the shape described. Leaving out some of the work, and only aiming to get it up in square shape as quickly as possible, I can put it up in an hour. The shanty as it should be, is shown in the illustration very fairly. And the shape of the cloth when spread out, is shown in the diagram on page 26. On the whole, it is the best form of close-side tent I have found. It admits of a bright fire in front, without which a forest camp is just no camp at all to me. I have suffered enough in close, dark, cheerless, damp tents.

More than thirty years ago I became disgusted with the clumsy, awkward, comfortless affairs that, under many different forms, went under the name of camps. Gradually I came to make a study of "camping out." It would take too much time and space, should I undertake to describe all the different styles and forms I have tried. But I will mention a few of the best and worst.

The old Down East "coal cabin" embodied the principle of the Indian camp. The frame was simply two strong crotches set firmly in the ground at a distance of eight feet apart, and interlocking at top. These supported a stiff ridge-pole fifteen feet long, the small end sharpened and set in the ground. Refuse boards, shooks, stakes, etc., were placed thickly from the ridge-pole to the ground; a thick layer of straw was laid over these, and the whole was covered a foot thick with earth and sods, well beaten down. A stone wall five feet high at back and sides made a most excellent fireplace; and these cabins were weather-proof and warm, even in zero weather. But they were too cumbersome, and included too much labor for the ordinary hunter and angler. Also, they were open to the objection, that while wide enough in front, they ran down to a dismal, cold peak at the far end. Remembering, however, the many pleasant winter nights I had passed with the coal-burners, I bought a supply of oil-cloth and rigged it on the same principle. It was a partial success, and I used it for one season. But that cold, peaked, dark space was always back of my head, and it seemed like an iceberg. It was in vain that I tied a handkerchief about my head, or drew a stocking-leg over it. That miserable, icy angle was always there. And it would only shelter one man anyhow. When winter drove me out of the woods I gave it to an enthusiastic young friend, bought some more oil-cloth, and commenced a shanty-tent that was meant to be perfect. A good many leisure hours were spent in cutting and sewing that shanty, which proved rather a success. It afforded a perfect shelter for a space 7x4 feet, but was a trifle heavy to pack, and the glazing began to crack and peel off in a short time. I made another and larger one of stout drilling, soaked in lime-water and alum; and this was all that could be asked when put up properly on a frame. But, the sides and ends being sewed to the roof made it unhandy to use as a shelter, when shelter was needed on short notice. So I ripped the back ends of the sides loose from the flap, leaving it, when spread out, as shown in the diagram. This was better; when it was necessary to make some sort of shelter in short order, it could be done with a single pole as used in the Indian camp, laying the tent across the pole, and using a few tacks to keep it in place at sides and center. This can be done in ten minutes, and makes a shelter-tent that will turn a heavy rain for hours.

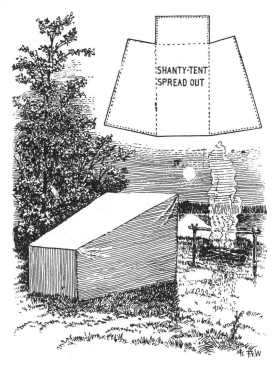

On the whole, for all kinds of weather, the shanty-tent is perhaps the best style of camp to be had at equal expense and trouble.

For a summer camp, however, I have finally come to prefer the simple lean-to or shed roof. It is the lightest, simplest and cheapest of all cloth devices for camping out, and I have found it sufficient for all weathers from June until the fall of the leaves. It is only a sheet of strong cotton cloth 9x7 feet, and soaked in lime and alum-water as the other. The only labor in making it is sewing two breadths of sheeting together. It needs no hemming, binding, loops or buttons, but is to be stretched on a frame as described for the brush shanty, and held in place with tacks. The one I have used for two seasons cost sixty cents, and weighs 2¼ pounds. It makes a good shelter for a party of three; and if it be found a little too breezy for cool nights, a sufficient windbreak can be made by driving light stakes at the sides and weaving in a siding of hemlock boughs.

Lastly, whatever cloth structure you may elect to use for a camp, do not fail to cover the roof with a screen of green boughs before building your camp-fire. Because there will usually be one fellow in camp who has a penchant for feeding the fire with old mulchy deadwood and brush, for the fun of watching the blaze, and the sparks that are prone to fly upward; forgetting that the blazing cinders are also prone to drop downward on the roof of the tent, burning holes in it.

I have spoken of some of the best camps I know. The worst ones are the A and wall tents, with all closed camps in which one is required to seclude himself through the hours of sleep in damp and darkness, utterly cut off from the cheerful, healthful light and warmth of the camp-fire.

Chapter IV

CAMP-FIRES AND THEIR IMPORTANCE—THE WASTE-
FUL WRONG WAY THEY ARE USUALLY MADE,
AND THE RIGHT WAY TO MAKE THEM

HARDLY second in importance to a warm, dry camp, is the camp-fire. In point of fact, the warmth, dryness, and healthfulness of a forest camp are mainly dependent on the way the fire is managed and kept up. No asthmatic or consumptive patient ever regained health by dwelling in a close, damp tent. I once camped for a week in a wall tent, with a Philadelphia party, and in cold weather. We had a little sheet iron fiend, called a camp-stove. When well fed with bark, knots and chips, it would get red hot, and, heaven knows, give out heat enough. By the time we were sound asleep, it would subside; and we would presently awake with chattering teeth to kindle her up again, take a smoke and a nip, turn in for another nap—to awaken again half frozen. It was a poor substitute for the open camp and bright fire. An experience of fifty years convinces me that a large percentage of the benefit obtained by invalids from camp life is attributable to the open camp and well-managed camp-fire. And the latter is usually handled in a way that is too sad, too wasteful; in short, badly botched. For instance.

It happened in the summer of '81 that I was making a canoe trip in the Northern Wilderness, and as Raquette Lake is the largest and about the most interesting lake in the North Woods, I spent about a week paddling, fishing, etc. I made my headquarters at Ed. Bennett's woodland hostelry, "Under the Hemlocks." As the hotel was filled with men, women and crying children, bitten to agony by punkies and mosquitoes, I chose to spread my blanket in a well-made bark shanty, which a signboard in black and white said was the "Guides' Camp."

And this camp was a very popular institution. Here it was that every evening, when night had settled down on forest and lake, the guests of the hotel would gather to lounge on the bed of fresh balsam browse, chat, sing and enjoy the huge camp-fire.

No woodland hotel will long remain popular that does not keep up a bright, cheery, out-o'-door fire. And the fun of it—to an old woodsman—is in noting how like a lot of school children they all act about the fire. Ed. Bennett had a man, a North Woods trapper, in his employ, whose chief business was to furnish plenty of wood for the guides' camp, and start a good fire every evening by sundown. As it grew dark and the blaze shone high and bright, the guests would begin to straggle in; and every man, woman and child seemed to view it as a religious duty to pause by the fire, and add a stick or two, before passing into camp. The wood was thrown on endwise, crosswise, or any way, so that it would burn, precisely as a crowd of boys make a bonfire on the village green. The object being, apparently, to get rid of the wood in the shortest possible time.

When the fire burnt low, toward mid-night, the guests would saunter off to the hotel; and the guides, who had been waiting impatiently, would organize what was left of the fire, roll themselves in their blankets, and turn in. I suggested to the trapper that he and I make one fire as it should be, and maybe they would follow suit—which would save half the fuel, with a better fire. But he said, "No; they like to build bonfires, and 'Ed.' can stand the wood, because it is best to let them have their own way. Time seems to hang heavy on their hands—and they pay well." Summer boarders, tourists and sportsmen, are not the only men who know how to build a camp-fire all wrong.

When I first came to Northern Pennsylvania, thirty-five years ago, I found game fairly abundant; and, as I wanted to learn the country where deer most abounded, I naturally cottoned to the local hunters. Good fellows enough, and conceited, as all local hunters and anglers are apt to be. Strong, good hunters and axe-men, to the manner born, and prone to look on any outsider as a tenderfoot. Their mode of building camp-fires was a constant vexation to me. They made it a point to always have a heavy sharp axe in camp, and toward night some sturdy chopper would cut eight or ten logs as heavy as the whole party could lug to camp with hand-spikes. The size of the logs was proportioned to the muscular force in camp. If there was a party of six or eight, the logs would be twice as heavy as when we were three or four. Just at dark, there would be a log heap built in front of the camp, well chinked with bark, knots and small sticks; and, for the next two hours, one could hardly get at the fire to light a pipe. But the fire was sure though slow. By 10 or 11 P. M. it would work its way to the front, and the camp would be warm and light. The party would turn in, and deep sleep would fall on a lot of tired hunters—for two or three hours. By which time some fellow near the middle was sure to throw his blanket off with a spiteful jerk, and dash out of camp with, "Holy Moses! I can't stand this; it's an oven."

Another Snorer (partially waking).—"N-r-r-rm, gu-r-r, ugh. Can't you—deaden—fire—a little?"

First Speaker.—"Deaden h——. If you want the fire deadened, get up and help throw off some of these logs."

Another (in coldest corner of shanty)—"What's 'er matter—with a-you fellows? Better dig out—an' cool off in the snow. Shanty's comfor'ble enough."

His minority report goes unheeded. The camp is roasted out. Strong hands and hand-spikes pry a couple of glowing logs from the front and replace them with two cold, green logs; the camp cools off, and the party takes to blankets once more —to turn out again at 5 A. M., and inaugurate breakfast. The fire is not in favorable shape for culinary operations, the heat is mainly on the back side, just where it isn't wanted. The few places level enough to set a pot or pan are too hot; and, in short, where there is any fire, there is too much. One man sees, with intense disgust, the nozzle of his coffee-pot drop into the fire. He makes a rash grab to save his coffee, and gets away —with the handle, which hangs on just enough to upset the pot.

"Old Al.," who is frying a slice of pork over a bed of coals that would melt a gun barrel, starts a horse laugh, that is cut short by a blue flash and an explosion of pork fat, which nearly blinds him. And the writer, taking in these mishaps in the very spirit of fun and frolic, is suddenly sobered and silenced by seeing his venison steak drop from the end of the "frizzling stick," and disappear between two glowing logs. The party manages, however, to get off on the hunt at daylight, with full stomachs; and perhaps the hearty fun and laughter more than compensate for these little mishaps.

This is a digression. But I am led to it by the recollection of many nights spent in camps and around camp-fires, pretty much as described above. I can smile today at the remembrance of the calm, superior way in which the old hunters of that day would look down on me, as from the upper branches of a tall hemlock, when I ventured to suggest that a better fire could be made with half the fuel and less than half the labor. They would kindly remark, "Oh, you are a Boston boy. You are used to paying $8.00 a cord for wood. We have no call to save wood here. We can afford to burn it by the acre." Which was more true than logical. Most of these men had commenced life with a stern declaration of war against the forest; and, although the men usually won at last, the battle was a long and hard one. Small wonder that they came to look upon a forest tree as a natural enemy. The camp-fire question came to a crisis, however, with two or three of these old settlers. And, as the story well illustrates my point, I will venture to tell it.

It was in the "dark days before Christmas" that a party of four started from W., bound for a camp on Second Fork, in the deepest part of the wilderness that lies between Wellsboro and the Block House. The party consisted of Sile J., Old Al., Eli J. and the writer. The two first were gray-haired men, the others past thirty; all the same, they called us "the boys." The weather was not inviting, and there was small danger of our camp being invaded by summer outers or tenderfeet. It cost twelve miles of hard travel to reach that camp; and, though we started at daylight, it was past noon when we arrived. The first seven miles could be made on wheels, the balance by hard tramping. The road was execrable; no one cared to ride; but it was necessary to have our loads carried as far as possible. The clearings looked dreary enough, and the woods forbidding to a degree, but our old camp was the picture of desolation. There was six inches of damp snow on the leafless brush roof, the blackened brands of our last fire were sticking their charred ends out of the snow, the hemlocks were bending sadly under their loads of wet snow, and the entire surroundings had a cold, cheerless, slushy look, very little like the ideal hunter's camp. We placed our knapsacks' in the shanty, Eli got out his nail hatchet, I drew my little pocket-axe, and we proceeded to start a fire, while the two older men went up stream a few rods to unearth a full-grown axe and a bottle of old rye, which they had cached under a log three months before. They never fooled with pocket-axes. They were gone so long that we sauntered up the band, thinking it might be the rye that detained them. We found them with their coats off, working like beavers, each with a stout, sharpened stick. There had been an October freshet, and a flood-jam at the bend had sent the mad stream over its banks, washing the log out of position and piling a gravel bar two feet deep over the spot where the axe and flask should have been. About the only thing left to do was to cut a couple of stout sticks, organize a mining company, limited, and go in; which they did. Sile was drifting into the side of the sandbar savagely, trying to strike the axe-helve, and Old Al. was sinking numberless miniature shafts from the surface in a vain attempt to strike whisky. The company failed in about half an hour. Sile resumed his coat, and sat down on a log—which was one of his best holds, by the way. He looked at Al.; Al. looked at him; then both looked at us, and Sile remarked that, if one of the boys wanted to go out to the clearings and "borry" an axe, and come back in the morning, he thought the others could pick up wood enough to tough it out one night. Of course nobody could stay in an open winter camp without an axe.

It was my time to come to the front. I said: "You two just go at the camp; clean the snow off and slick up the inside. Put my shelter-cloth with Eli's, and cover the roof with them; and if you don't have just as good a fire tonight as you ever had, you can tie me to a beech and leave me here. Come on, Eli." And Eli did come on. And this is how we did it: We first felled a thrifty butternut tree ten inches in diameter, cut off three lengths at five feet each, and carried them to camp. These were

the back logs. Two stout stakes were driven at the back of the
fire, and the logs, on top of each other, were laid firmly against
the stakes. The latter were slanted a little back, and the largest
log placed at bottom, the smallest on top, to prevent tipping
forward. A couple of short, thick sticks were laid with the ends
against the bottom log by way of fire dogs; a fore stick, five feet
long and five inches in diameter; a well built pyramid of bark,
knots and small logs completed the camp-fire, which sent a pleasant glow of warmth and heat to the furthest corner of the
shanty. For "night-wood," we cut a dozen birch and ash poles
from four to six inches across, trimmed them to the tips, and
dragged them to camp. Then we denuded a dry hemlock of its
bark by the aid of ten-foot poles, flattened at one end, and

CAMP-FIRE AS IT SHOULD BE MADE

packed the bark to camp. We had a bright, cheery fire from
the early evening until morning, and four tired hunters never
slept more soundly.

We stayed in that camp a week; and, though the weather was
rough and cold, the little pocket-axes kept us well in firewood.
We selected butternut for backlogs, because, when green, it
burns very slowly and lasts a long time. And we dragged our
smaller wood to camp in lengths of twenty to thirty feet, because it was easier to lay them on the fire and burn them
in two than to cut them shorter with light hatchets. With a
heavy axe, we should have cut them to lengths of five or six
feet.

Our luck, I may mention, was good—as good as we desired.
Not that four smallish deer are anything to brag about for a

week's hunt by four men and two dogs. I have known a pot-hunter to kill nine in a single day. But we had enough.

As it was, we were obliged to "double trip it" in order to get our deer and duffle down to "Babb's." And we gave away more than half our venison. For the rest, the illustrations show the camp-fire—all but the fire—as it should be made.

Chapter V

FISHING, WITH AND WITHOUT FLIES—SOME TACKLE
AND LURES—DISCURSIVE REMARKS ON THE GENTLE
ART—THE HEADLIGHT—FROGGING

 HERE is probably no subject connected with outdoor sport so thoroughly and exhaustively written up as fly-fishing, and all that pertains thereto. Fly-fishing for speckled trout always, and deservedly, takes the lead. Bass fishing usually comes next, though some writers accord second place to the lake trout, salmon trout or land-locked salmon. The mascalonge, as a game fish, is scarcely behind the small-mouthed bass, and is certainly more gamy than the lake trout. The large-mouthed bass and pickerel are usually ranked about with the yellow perch. I don't know why; they are certainly gamy enough. Perhaps it is because they do not leap out of water when hooked. Both are good on the table.

A dozen able and interesting authors have written books wherein trout, flies and fly-fishing are treated in a manner that leaves an old backwoodsman little to say. Rods, reels, casting lines, flies and fish are described and descanted on in a way, and in a language, the reading whereof reduces me to temporary insanity. And yet I seem to recollect some bygone incidents concerning fish and fishing. I have a well-defined notion that I once stood on Flat Rock, in Big Pine Creek, and caught over 350 fine trout in a short day's fishing. Also that many times I left home on a bright May or June morning, walked eight miles, caught a twelve-pound creel of trout, and walked home before bedtime.

I remember that once, in Michigan, on the advice of local fishermen, I dragged a spoon around High Bank Lake two days, with little result save half a dozen blisters on my hands; and that on the next morning, taking a long tamarack pole and my own way of fishing, I caught, before 10 A. M., fifty pounds of bass and pickerel, weighing from two to ten pounds each.

Gibson, whose spoon, line and skiff I had been using and who was the fishing oracle of that region, could hardly believe his eyes. I kept that country inn, and the neighborhood as well, supplied with fish for the next two weeks.

It is truth to say that I have never struck salt or fresh waters, where edible fish were at all plentiful, without being able to take, in some way, all that I needed. Notably and preferably with the fly if that might be. If not, then with worms, grubs, minnows, grasshoppers, crickets, or any sort of doodle bug their highnesses might affect. When a plump, two-pound trout refuses to eat a tinseled, feathered fraud, I am not the man to refuse him something more edible.

That I may not be misunderstood, let me say that I recognized the speckled brook trout as the very emperor of all game fish, and angling for him with the fly as the neatest, most fascinating sport attainable by the angler. But there are thousands of outers who, from choice or necessity, take their summer vacations where *Salmo fontinalis* is not to be had. They would prefer him, either on the leader or the table; but he is not there; "And a man has got a stomach, and we live by what we eat."

Wherefore, they go a-fishing for other fish. So that they are successful and sufficiently fed, the difference is not so material. I have enjoyed myself hugely catching catties on a dark night from a skiff with a hand-line.

I can add nothing in a scientific way to the literature of fly-fishing; but I can give a few hints that may be conducive to practical success, as well with trout as with less noble fish. In fly-fishing, one serviceable four-ounce rod is enough; and a plain click reel, of small size, is just as satisfactory as a more costly affair. Twenty yards of tapered, water-proof line, with a six-foot leader, and a cost of two flies, complete the rig, and will be found sufficient. In common with most fly-fishers, I have mostly thrown a cast of three flies, but have found two just as effective, and handier.

We all carry too many flies. Some of my friends have more than sixty dozen, and will never use a tenth of them. In the summer of '88, finding I had more than seemed needful, I left all but four dozen behind me. I wet only fifteen of them in a seven weeks' outing. And they filled the bill. I have no time or space for a dissertation on the hundreds of different flies made and sold at the present day. Abler pens have done that. I will, however, name a few that I have found good in widely different localities, i.e., the Northern Wilderness of New York and the upper waters of Northern Pennsylvania. For the Northern Wilderness: Scarlet ibis, split ibis, Romeyn, white-winged coachman, royal coachman, red hackle, red-bodied ashy and gray-bodied ashy. The ashies were good for black bass also. For Northern Pennsylvania: Queen of the waters, professor, red fox, coachman, black may, white-winged coachman, wasp, brown hackle, Seth Green. Ibis flies are worthless here. Using the dark flies in bright water and clear weather, and the brighter colors for evening, the list was long enough.

At the commencement of the open season, and until the young maple leaves are half grown, bait will be be found far more successful than the fly. At this time the trout are pretty evenly distributed along lake shores and streams, choosing to lie quietly in rather deep pools, and avoiding swift water. A few may rise to the fly in a logy, indifferent way; but the best way to take them is bait-fishing with well-cleansed angle-worms or white grubs, the latter being the best bait I have ever tried. They take the bait sluggishly at this season, but, on feeling the hook, wake up to their normal activity and fight gamely to the last. When young, new-born insects begin to drop freely on the water about the 20th of May, trout leave the pools and take to the riffles. And from this time until the latter part of June the fly-fisherman is in his glory. It may be true that the skillful bait-fisherman will rather beat his creel. He cares not for that. He can take enough; and he had rather take ten trout with the fly than a score with bait. As for the man who goes a-fishing simply to catch fish, the fly-fisher does not recognize him as an angler at all.

When the sun is hot and the weather grows warm, trout leave
the ripples and take to cold springs and spring-holes; the largest fish, of course, monopolizing the deepest and coolest places,
while the smaller ones hover around, or content themselves
with shallower water. As the weather gets hotter, the fly-fishing
falls off badly. A few trout of four to eight ounces in weight
may still be raised, but the larger ones are lying on the bottom, and are not to be fooled with feathers. They will take a
tempting bait when held before their noses—sometimes; at other
times, not. As to raising them with a fly—as well attempt to
raise a sick Indian with the temperance pledge. And yet, they
may be taken in bright daylight by a ruse that I learned long
ago, of a youngster less than half my age, a little, freckled,
thin-visaged young man, whose health was evidently affected
by a daily struggle with a pair of tow-colored side whiskers and
a light mustache. There was hardly enough of the whole affair
to make a door-mat for a bee hive. But he seemed so proud of
the plant, that I forebore to rig him. He was better than he
looked—as often happens. The landlord said, "He brings in
large trout every day, when our best fly-fishermen fail." One
night, around an out-door fire, we got acquainted, and I found
him a witty, pleasant companion. Before turning in I ventured
to ask him how he succeeded in taking large trout, while the
experts only caught small ones, or failed altogether.

"Go with me tomorrow morning to a spring-hole three miles
up the river, and I'll show you," he said.

Of course, we went. He, rowing a light skiff, and I paddling
a still lighter canoe. The spring-hole was in a narrow bay that
set back from the river, and at the mouth of a cold, clear brook;
it was ten to twelve feet deep, and at the lower end a large
balsam had fallen in with the top in just the right place for
getting away with large fish, or tangling lines and leaders. We
moored some twenty feet above the spring-hole, and commenced
fishing, I with my favorite cast of flies, my friend with the tail
of a minnow. He caught a 1½-pound trout almost at the out-
set, but I got no rise; did not expect it. Then I went above,
where the water was shallower, and raised a couple of half-
pounders, but could get no more. I thought he had better go
to the hotel with what he had, but my friend said "wait"; he

went ashore and picked up a long pole with a bushy tip; it had evidently been used before. Dropping down to the spring-hole, he thrust the tip to the bottom and slashed it around in a way to scare and scatter every trout within a hundred feet.

"And what does all that mean?" I asked.

"Well," he said, "every trout will be back in less than an hour; and when they first come back, they take the bait greedily. Better take off your leader and try bait."

Which I did. Dropping our hooks to the bottom, we waited some twenty minutes, when he had a bite, and, having strong tackle, soon took in a trout that turned the scale at 2¼ pounds. Then my turn came and I saved one weighing 1½ pounds. He caught another of 1¼ pounds, and I took one of 1 pound. Then they ceased biting altogether.

"And now," said my friend, "if you will work your canoe carefully around to that old balsam top and get the light where you can see the bottom, you may see some large trout."

I did as directed, and, making a telescope of my hand, looked intently for the bottom of the spring-hole. At first I could see nothing but water; then I made out some dead sticks, and finally began to dimly trace the outlines of large fish. There they were, more than forty of them, lying quietly on the bottom like suckers, but genuine brook trout, every one of them.

"This," said he, "makes the fifth time I have brushed them out of here, and I have never missed taking from two to five large trout. I have two other places where I always get one or two, but this is the best."

At the hotel we found two fly-fishers who had been out all the morning. They each had three or four small trout.

During the next week we worked the spring-holes daily in the same way, and always with success. I have also had good success by building a bright fire on the bank, and fishing a spring-hole by the light—a mode of fishing especially successful with catties and perch.

A bright, bull's-eye headlight, strapped on a stiff hat, so that the light can be thrown where it is wanted, is an excellent device for night fishing. And during the heated term, when fish are slow and sluggish, I have found the following plan works well: Bake a hard, well salted, water "johnny-cake," break it into pieces the size of a hen's egg, and drop the pieces into a spring-hole. This calls a host of minnows, and the larger fish follow the minnows. It will prove more successful on perch, catties, chubs, etc., than on trout, however. By this plan, I have kept a camp of five men well supplied with fish when their best flies failed—as they mostly do in very hot weather.

Fishing for mascalonge, pickerel, and bass, is quite another thing, though by many valued as a sport scarcely inferior to fly-fishing for trout. I claim no especial skill with the fly-rod. It is a good day when I get my tail fly more than fifteen yards beyond the reel, with any degree of accuracy.

My success lies mainly with the tribes of Esox and Micropterus. Among these, I have seldom or never failed during the last thirty-six years, when the water was free of ice; and I have had just as good luck when big-mouthed bass and pickerel were in the "off season," as at any time. For in many waters there comes a time—in late August and September—when neither bass nor pickerel will notice the spoon, be it handled never so wisely. Even the mascalonge looks on the flashing cheat with indifference; though a very hungry specimen may occasionally immolate himself. It was at such a season that I fished High Bank Lake—as before mentioned—catching from forty to fifty pounds of fine fish every morning for nearly two weeks, after the best local fishermen had assured me that not a decent sized fish could be taken at that season. Perhaps a brief description of the modes and means that have proved invariably successful for many years may afford a few useful hints, even to old anglers.

To begin with, I utterly discard all modern "gangs" and "trains," carrying from seven to thirteen hooks each. They are all too small, and all too many; better calculated to scratch and tear, than to catch and hold. Three hooks are enough at the end of any line, and better than more. These should be fined or honed to a perfect point, and the abrupt part of the barb filed down one-half. All hooks, as usually made, have twice as much barb as they should have; and the sharp bend of the barb prevents the entering of the hook in hard bony structures, wherefore the fish only stays hooked so long as there is a taut pull on the line. A little loosening of the line and shake of the head sets him free. But no fish can shake out a hook well sunken in mouth or gills, though two-thirds of the barb be filed away.

For mascalonge or pickerel I invariably use wire snells made as follows: Lay off four or more strands of fine brass wire 13 inches long; turn one end of the wires smoothly over a No. 1 iron wire, and work the ends in between the strands below. Now, with a pair of pincers hold the ends, and, using No. 1 as a handle, twist the ends and body of the snell firmly together; this gives the loop; next, twist the snell evenly and strongly from end to

FROG-BAIT   THREE-HOOK GANG

end. Wax the end of the snell thoroughly for two or three inches, and wax the tapers of two strong Sproat or O'Shaughnessy hooks, and wind the lower hook on with strong, waxed silk, to the end of the taper; then lay the second hook at right angles with the first, and one inch above it; wind this as the other, and then fasten a third and smaller hook above that for a lip hook. This gives the snell about one foot in length, with the two lower hooks standing at right angles, one above the other, and a third and smaller hook in line with the second.

The bait is the element of success; it is made as follows: Slice off a clean, white pork rind, four or five inches long by an inch and a half wide; lay it on a board, and, with a sharp knife cut it as nearly to the shape of a frog as your ingenuity permits. Prick a slight gash in the head to admit the lip hook, which should be an inch and a half above the second one, and see that the fork of the bait rests securely in the barb of the middle hook.

Use a stout bait-rod and a strong line. Fish from a boat, with a second man to handle the oars, if convenient. Let the oarsman lay the boat ten feet inside the edge of the lily-pads, and make your cast, say, with thirty feet of line; land the bait neatly to the right, at the edge of the lily-pads, let it sink a few inches, and then with the tip well lowered, bring the bait around on a slight curve by a quick succession of draws, with a momentary pause between each; the object being to imitate as nearly as possible a swimming frog. If this be neatly done, and if the bait be made as it should be, at every short halt the legs will spread naturally, and the imitation is perfect enough to deceive the most experienced bass or pickerel. When half a dozen casts to right and left have been made without success, it is best to move on, still keeping inside and casting outside the lily-pads.

A pickerel of three pounds or more will take in all three hooks at the first snap; and, as he closes his mouth tightly and starts for the bottom, strike quickly, but not too hard, and let the boatman put you out into deep water at once, where you are safe from the strong roots of the yellow lily.

It is logically certain your fish is well hooked. You cannot pull two strong, sharp hooks through that tightly closed mouth without fastening at least one of them where it will do most good. Oftener both will catch, and it frequently happens that one hook will catch each lip, holding the mouth nearly closed, and shortening the struggles of a large fish very materially. On taking off a fish, and before casting again, see that the two lower hooks stand at right angles. If they have got turned in the struggle you can turn them at any angle you like; the twisted wire is stiff enough to hold them in place. Every angler knows the bold, determined manner in which the mascalonge strikes his prey. He will take in bait and hooks at the first dash, and if the rod be held stiffly usually hooks himself. Barring large trout, he is the king of game fish. The big-mouthed bass is less savage in his attacks, but is a free biter. He is apt to come up behind and seize the bait about two-thirds of its length, turn, and bore down for the bottom. He will mostly take in the lower hooks, however, and is certain to get fastened. His large mouth is excellent for retaining the hook.

As for the small-mouthed (*Micropterus dolomieu,* if you want to be scientific), I have found him more capricious than any game fish on the list. One day he will take only dobsons, or crawfish; the next, he may prefer minnows, and again, he will rise to the fly or a bucktail spinner.

On the whole, I have found the pork frog the most successful lure in his case; but the hooks and bait must be arranged differently. Three strands of fine wire will make a snell strong enough, and the hooks should be strong, sharp and rather small, the lower hooks placed only half an inch apart, and a small lip hook two and a quarter inches above the middle one. As the fork of the bait will not reach the bend of the middle hook, it must be fastened to the snell by a few stitches taken with stout thread, and the lower end of the bait should not reach more than a quarter of an inch beyond the bottom of the hook, because the small-mouth has a villainous trick of giving his prey a stern chase, nipping constantly and viciously at the tail, and the above arrangement will be apt to hook him at the first snap. Owing to this trait, some artificial minnows with one or two hooks at the caudal end, are very killing—when he will take them.

Lake, or salmon trout, may be trolled for successfully with the above lure; but I do not much affect fishing for them. Excellent sport may be had with them, however, early in the season, when they are working near the shore, but they soon retire to water from fifty to seventy feet deep, and can only be caught by deep trolling or buoy-fishing. I have no fancy for sitting in a slow-moving boat for hours, dragging three or four hundred feet of line in deep water, a four-pound sinker tied by six feet of lighter line some twenty feet above the hooks. The sinker is supposed to go bumping along the bottom, while the bait follows three or four feet above it. The drag of the line and the constant joggling of the sinker on rocks and snags, make it difficult to tell when one has a strike—and it is always too long between bites.

Sitting for hours at a baited buoy with a hand-line, and without taking a fish, is still worse, as more than once I have been compelled to acknowledge in very weariness of soul. There are enthusiastic anglers, however, whose specialty is trolling for lake trout. A gentleman by the name of Thatcher, who has a fine residence on Raquette Lake—which he calls a camp—makes this his leading sport, and keeps a log of his fishing, putting nothing on record of less than ten pounds weight. His largest fish was booked at twenty-eight pounds, and he added that a well-conditioned salmon trout was superior to a brook trout on the table; in which I quite agree with him. But he seemed quite disgusted when I ventured to suggest that a well-conditioned cattie or bullhead, caught in the same waters—was better than either.

"Do you call the cattie a game fish?" he asked.

Yes; I call any fish a game fish that is taken for sport with hook and line. I can no more explain the common prejudice against the catfish and eel than I can tell why an experienced angler should drag a gang of thirteen hooks through the water—ten of them being worse than superfluous. "Frank Forester" gives five hooks as the number for a trolling gang. We mostly use hooks too small, and do not look after points and barbs closely enough. A pair of No. 1 O'Shaughnessy, or 1½ Sproat, or five tapered blackfish hooks, will make a killing rig for small-mouthed bass using No. 4 Sproat for lip hook. Larger hooks are better for the big-mouthed, a four-pound specimen of which will easily take in one's fist. A pair of 5-0 O'Shaughnessy's, or Sproat's will be found none too large; and as for the mascalonge and pickerel, if I must err, let it be on the side of large hooks and strong lines.

It is idle to talk of playing the fish in water where the giving of a few yards insures a hopeless tangle among roots, tree-tops, etc. I was once fishing in Western waters where the pickerel ran very large, and I used a pair of the largest salmon hooks with tackle strong enough to hold a fish of fifteen pounds, without any playing; notwithstanding which, I had five trains of three hooks each taken off in as many days by monster pickerel. An expert mascalonge fisherman—Davis by name—happened to take board at the farm house where I was staying, and he had a notion that he could "beat some of them big fellows;" and he did it; with three large cod hooks, a bit of fine, strong chain, twelve yards of cod-line, an eighteen-foot tamarack pole, and a twelve inch sucker for bait. I thought it the most outlandish rig I had ever seen, but went with him in the early gray of the morning to see it tried, just where I had lost my hooks and fish.

Raising the heavy bait in the air, he would give it a whirl to gather headway, and launch it forty feet away with a splash that might have been heard thirty rods. It looked more likely to scare than catch, but was a success. At the third or fourth cast we plainly saw a huge pickerel rise, shut his immense mouth over bait, hooks, and a few inches of chain, turn lazily, and head for the bottom, where Mr. D. let him rest a minute, and then struck steadily but strongly. The subsequent struggle depended largely on main strength, though there was a good deal of skill and cool judgment shown in the handling and landing of the fish. A pickerel of forty pounds or more is not to be snatched out of the water on his first mad rush; something must be yielded—and with no reel there is little chance of giving line. It struck me my friend managed his fish remarkably well, towing him back and forth with a strong pull, never giving him a rest and finally sliding him out on a low muddy bank, as though he were a smooth log. We took him up to the house and tested the size of his mouth by putting a quart cup in it, which went in easily. Then we weighed him, and he turned the scales at forty-four pounds. It was some consolation to find three of my hooks sticking in his mouth. Lastly, we had a large section of him stuffed and baked. It was good; but a ten-pound fish would have been better. The moral of all this—if it has any moral—is, use hooks according to the size of fish you expect to catch.

And, when you are in a permanent camp, and fishing is very poor, try frogging. It is not a sport of a high order, though it may be called angling—and it can be made amusing, with hook and line. I have seen educated ladies in the wilderness, fishing for frogs with an eagerness and enthusiasm not surpassed by the most devoted angler with his favorite cast of flies.

There are several modes of taking the festive batrachian. He is speared with a frog-spear; caught under the chin with snatch-hooks; taken with hook and line, or picked up from a canoe with the aid of a headlight, or jack-lamp. The two latter modes are best.

To take him with hook and line: a light rod, six to eight feet of line, a snell of single gut with a 1-0 Sproat or O'Shaughnessy hook, and a bit of bright scarlet flannel for bait; this is the rig. To use it, paddle up behind him silently, and drop the rag just in front of his nose. He is pretty certain to take it on the instant. Knock him on the head before cutting off his legs. It is unpleasant to see him squirm, and hear him cry like a child while you are sawing at his thigh joints.

By far the most effective manner of frogging is by the headlight on dark nights. To do this most successfully, one man in a light canoe, a good headlight and a light, one-handed paddle, are the requirements. The frog is easily located, either by his croaking, or by his peculiar shape. Paddle up to him silently and throw the light in his eyes; you may then pick him up as you would a potato. I have known a North Woods guide to pick up a five-quart pail of frogs in an hour, on a dark evening. On the table, frogs' legs are usually conceded first place for delicacy and flavor. For an appetizing breakfast in camp, they have no equal, in my judgment. The high price they bring at the best hotels, and their growing scarcity, attest the value placed on them by men who know how and what to eat. And, not many years ago, an old pork-gobbling backwoodsman threw his frying-pan into the river because I had cooked frogs' legs in it. While another, equally intelligent, refused to use my frying-pan, because I had cooked eels in it; remarking sententiously, "Eels is snakes, an' I know it."

It may be well, just here and now, to say a word on the importance of the headlight. I know of no more pleasant and satisfactory adjunct of a camp than a good light that can be adjusted to the head, used as a jack in floating, carried in the hand, or fastened up inside the shanty. Once fairly tried, it will never be ignored or forgotten. Not that it will show a deer's head seventeen rods distant with sufficient clearness for a shot—or your sights with distinctness enough to make it. (See Murray's *Adirondacks*, page 174.)

A headlight that will show a deer plainly at six rods, while lighting the sights of a rifle with clearness, is an exceptionally good light. More deer are killed in floating under than over four rods. There are various styles of headlights, jack-lamps, etc., in use. They are bright, easily adjusted, and will show rifle sights, or a deer, up to 100 feet—which is enough. They are also convenient in camp, and better than a lantern on a dim forest path.

Before leaving the subject of bait-fishing, I have a point or two I wish to make. I have attempted to explain the frog-bait, and the manner of using it, and I shall probably never have occasion to change my belief that it is, on the whole, the most killing lure for the entire tribes of bass and pickerel. There is however, another, which, if properly handled, is almost as good. It is as follows:

Take a bass, pickerel, or yellow perch, of one pound or less; scrape the scales clean on the under side from the caudal fin to a point just forward of the vent.

Next, with a sharp knife, cut up toward the backbone, commencing just behind the vent with a slant toward the tail. Run the knife smoothly along just under the backbone, and out through the caudal fin, taking about one-third of the latter, and making a clean, white bait, with the anal and part of the caudal by way of fins. It looks very like a white minnow in the water; but is better, in that it is more showy, and infinitely tougher. A minnow soon drags to pieces. To use it, two strong hooks are tied on a wire snell at right angles, the upper one an inch above the lower, and the upper hook is passed through the bait, leaving it to draw without turning or spinning. The casting and handling is the same as with the frog-bait, and is very killing for bass, pickerel, and mascalonge. It is a good lure for salmon trout also; but, for him it was found better to fasten the bait with the lower hook in a way to give it a spinning motion; and this necessitates the use of a swivel, which I do not like; because, "a rope is as strong as its weakest part"; and I have more than once found that weakest part the swivel. If, however, a swivel has been tested by a dead lift of twenty to twenty-five pounds, it will do to trust.

I have spoken only of brass or copper wire for snells, and for pickerel or mascalonge of large size nothing else is to be depended on. But for trout and bass, strong gut or gimp is safe enough. The possibilities as to size of the mascalonge and Northern pickerel no man knows. Frank Forester thinks it probable that the former attains to the weight of sixty to eighty pounds, while he only accords the pickerel a weight of seventeen to eighteen pounds. I have seen several pickerel of over forty pounds, and one that turned the scale at fifty-three. And I saw a mascalonge on Georgian Bay that was longer than the Canuck guide who was toting the fish over his shoulder by a stick thrust in the mouth and gills. The snout reached to the top of the guide's head, while the caudal fin dragged on the ground. There was no chance for weighing the fish, but I hefted him several times, carefully, and am certain he weighed more than a bushel of wheat. Just what tackle would be proper for such a powerful fellow I am not prepared to say, having lost the largest specimens I ever hooked. My best mascalonge weighed less than twenty pounds. My largest pickerel still less.

I will close this discursive chapter by offering a bit of advice. Do not go into the woods on a fishing tour without a stock of well cleansed angle-worms. Keep them in a tin can partly filled with damp moss, and in a cool moist place. There is no one variety of bait that the angler finds so constantly useful as the worm. Izaak Walton by no means despised worm or bait-fishing.

Chapter VI

CAMP COOKERY—HOW IT IS USUALLY DONE, WITH A
FEW SIMPLE HINTS ON PLAIN COOKING—COOKING
FIRE AND OUT-DOOR RANGE

HE way in which an average party of summer
outers will contrive to manage—or mis-manage—the
camp and camp-fire so as to get the greatest amount
of smoke and discontent at the least outlay of time
and force, is something past all understanding, and
somewhat aggravating to an old woodsman who
knows some better. But it is just as good fun as the
cynical O. W. can ask, to see a party of three or four
enthusiastic youngsters organize the camp on the first day in,
and proceed to cook the first meal. Of course, every man is boss,
and every one is bound to build the fire, which every one proceeds to do. There are no back logs, no fore sticks, and no
arrangement for level solid bases on which to place frying-pans,
coffee pots, etc. But, there is a sufficiency of knots, dry sticks,
bark and chunks, with some kindling at the bottom, and a heavy
volume of smoke working its way through the awkward-looking
pile. Presently thin tongues of blue flame begin to shoot up
through the interstices, and four brand new coffee pots are
wriggled into level positions at as many different points on the
bonfire. Four hungry youngsters commence slicing ham and pork,
four frying-pans are brought out from as many hinged and lid-
ded soap boxes—when one man yells out hurriedly, "Look out,
Joe, there's your coffee pot handle coming off." And he drops
his frying-pan to save his coffee pot, which he does, minus the
spout and handle. Then it is seen that the flames have increased

rapidly, and all the pots are in danger. A short, sharp skirmish rescues them, at the expense of some burned fingers, and culinary operations are the order of the hour.

Coffee and tea are brewed with the loss of a handle or two, and the frying-pans succeed in scorching the pork and ham to an unwholesome black mess. The potato kettle does better. It is not easy to spoil potatoes by cooking them in plenty of boiling water; and, as there is plenty of bread with fresh butter, not to mention canned goods, the hungry party feed sufficiently, but not satisfactorily. Everything seems pervaded with smoke. The meat is scorched bitter, and the tea is of the sort described by Charles Dudley Warner, in his humorous description of "Camping Out": "The sort of tea that takes hold, lifts the hair, and disposes the drinker to hilariousness. There is no deception about it, it tastes of tannin, and spruce, and creosote." Of the cooking he says: "Everything has been cooked in a tin pail and a skillet—potatoes, tea, pork, mutton, slapjacks. You wonder how everything would have been prepared in so few utensils. When you eat, the wonder ceases, everything might have been cooked in one pail. It is a noble meal. . . . The slapjacks are a solid job of work, made to last, and not go to pieces in a person's stomach like a trivial bun."

I have before me a copy of *Forest and Stream,* in which the canoe editor, under the heading of "The Galley Fire," has some remarks well worth quoting. He says: "The question of camp cookery is one of the greatest importance to all readers of *Forest and Stream,* but most of all to the canoeists. From ignorance of what to carry the canoeist falls back on canned goods, never healthy as a steady diet, Brunswick soup and eggs. . . . The misery of that first camp-fire, who has forgotten it? Tired, hungry, perhaps cold and wet, the smoke everywhere, the coffee pot melted down, the can of soup upset in the fire, the fiendish conduct of frying-pan and kettle, the final surrender of the exhausted victim, sliding off to sleep with a piece of hardtack in one hand and a slice of canned beef in the other, only to dream of mother's hot biscuits, juicy steaks, etc., etc." It is very well put, and so true to the life. And again: "Frying, baking, making coffee, stews, plain biscuits, the neat and speedy preparation of a healthy 'square meal' can be easily learned." Aye, and should

be learned by every man who goes to the woods with or without
a canoe.

But I was describing a first day's camping out, the party being
four young men and one old woodsman, the latter going along in
a double character of invited guest and amateur guide. When the
boys are through with their late dinner, they hustle the greasy
frying-pans and demoralized tinware into a corner of the shanty,
and get out their rods for an evening's fishing. They do it
hurriedly, almost feverishly, as youngsters are apt to do at the
start. The O. W. has taken no part in the dinner, and has said
nothing save in response to direct questions, nor has he done
anything to keep up his reputation as a woodsman, except to see
that the shelter roof is properly put up and fastened. Having
seen to this, he reverts to his favorite pastime, sitting on a log
and smoking navy plug. Long experience has taught him that it
is best to let the boys effervesce a little. They will slop over a
trifle at first, but twenty-four hours will settle them. When they
are fairly out of hearing, he takes the old knapsack from the
clipped limb where it has been hung, cuts a slice of ham, butters
a slice of bread, spreads the live coals and embers, makes a pot
of strong green tea, broils the ham on a three-pronged birch
fork, and has a clean, well-cooked plain dinner. Then he takes
the sharp three-pound camp axe, and fells a dozen small birch
and ash trees, cutting them into proper lengths and leaving them
for the boys to tote into camp. Next, a bushy, heavy-topped
hemlock is felled, and the O. W. proceeds leisurely to pick a
heap of fine hemlock browse. A few handfuls suffice to stuff the
muslin pillow bag, and the rest is carefully spread on the port
side of the shanty for a bed. The pillow is placed at the head,
and the old Mackinac blanket-bag is spread neatly over all, as a
token of ownership and possession. If the youngsters want beds
of fine, elastic browse, let 'em make their own beds.

No camp-fire should be without poker and tongs. The poker
is a beech stick four feet long by two inches thick, flattened at
one end, with a notch cut in it for lifting kettles, etc. To make
the tongs, take a tough beech or hickory stick, one inch thick by
two feet in length, shave it down nearly one-half for a foot in the
center, thrust this part into hot embers until it bends freely,
bring the ends together and whittle them smoothly to a fit on

the inside, cross-checking them also to give them a grip; finish off by chamfering the ends neatly from the outside. They will be found exceedingly handy in rescuing a bit of tinware, a slice of steak or ham, or any small article that happens to get dropped in a hot fire.

And don't neglect the camp broom. It is made by laying bushy hemlock twigs around a light handle, winding them firmly with strong twine or moose wood bark, and chopping off the ends of the twigs evenly. It can be made in ten minutes. Use it to brush any leaves, sticks, and any litter from about the camp or fire. Neatness is quite as pleasant and wholesome around the forest camp as in the home kitchen. These little details may seem trivial to the reader. But remember, if there is a spot on earth where trifles make up the sum of human enjoyment, it is to be found in a woodland camp. All of which the O. W. fully appreciates, as he finishes the above little jobs; after which he proceeds to spread the fire to a broad level bed of glowing embers, nearly covering the same with small pieces of hemlock bark, that the boys may have a decent cooking fire on their return.

About sundown they come straggling in, not jubilant and hilarious, footsore rather and a little cross. The effervescence is subsiding, and the noise is pretty well knocked out of them. They have caught and dressed some three score of small brook trout, which they deposit beside the shanty, and proceed at once to move on the fire, with evident intent of raising a conflagration, but are checked by the O. W., who calls their attention to the fact that for all culinary purposes, the fire is about as near the right thing as they are likely to get it. Better defer the bonfire until after supper. Listening to the voice of enlightened woodcraft, they manage to fry trout and make tea without scorch or creosote, and the supper is a decided improvement on the dinner. But the dishes are piled away as before, without washing.

Then follows an hour of busy work, bringing wood to camp and packing browse. The wood is sufficient; but the browse is picked, or cut, all too coarse, and there is only enough of it to make the camp look green and pleasant—not enough to rest weary shoulders and backs. But, they are sound on the bonfire. They pile on the wood in the usual way, criss-cross and haphazard. It makes a grand fire, and lights up the forest for fifty yards around, and the tired youngsters turn in. Having the advantage of driving a team to the camping ground, they are well supplied with blankets and robes. They ought to sleep soundly, but they don't. The usual drawbacks of a first night in camp are soon manifested in uneasy twistings and turnings, grumbling at stubs, knots, and sticks, that utterly ignore conformity with the angles of the human frame. But at last, tired nature asserts her supremacy, and they sleep. Sleep soundly, for a couple of hours; when the bonfire, having reached the point of disintegration, suddenly collapses with a sputtering and crackling that brings them to their head's antipodes, and four dazed, sleepy faces look out with a bewildered air, to see what has caused the rumpus. All take a hand in putting the brands together and re-arranging the fire, which burns better than at first; some sleepy talk, one or two feeble attempts at a smoke, and they turn in again. But, there is not an hour during the remainder of the night in which some one is not pottering about the fire.

The O.W., who has abided by his blanket-bag all night—quietly taking in the fun—rouses out the party at 4 A. M. For two of them are to fish Asaph Run with bait, and the other two are to try the riffles of Marsh Creek with the fly. As the wood is all burned to cinders and glowing coals, there is no chance for a smoky fire; and, substituting coffee for tea, the breakfast is a repetition of the supper.

By sunrise the boys are off, and the O. W. has the camp to himself. He takes it leisurely, gets up a neat breakfast of trout, bread, butter, and coffee, cleans and puts away his dishes, has a smoke, and picks up the camp axe. Selecting a bushy hemlock fifteen inches across, he lets it down in as many minutes, trims it to the very tip, piles the limbs in a heap, and cuts three lengths of six feet each from the butt. This insures browse and back logs for some time ahead. Two strong stakes are cut and sharpened. Four small logs, two of eight and two of nine feet in length, are prepared, plenty of night wood is made ready, a supply of bright, dry hemlock bark is carried to camp, and the O. W. rests from his labors, resuming his favorite pastime of sitting on a log and smoking navy plug. Finally it occurs to him that he is there partly as guide and mentor to the younger men, and that they need a lesson on cleanliness. He brings out the frying-pans and finds a filthy-looking mess of grease in each one, wherein ants, flies, and other insects have contrived to get mixed. Does he heat some water, and clean and scour the pans? Not if he knows himself. If he did it once he might keep on doing it. He is cautious about establishing precedents, and he has a taste for entomology. He places the pans in the sun where the grease will soften and goes skirmishing for ants and doodle bugs. They are not far to seek, and he soon has a score of large black ants, with a few bugs and spiders, pretty equally distributed among the frying-pans. To give the thing a plausible look a few flies are added, and the two largest pans are finished off, one with a large earwig, the other with a thousand-legged worm. The pans are replaced in the shanty, the embers are leveled and nearly covered with bits of dry hemlock bark, and the O. W. resumes his pipe and log

> With such a face of Christian satisfaction,
> As good men wear, who have done a virtuous action.

Before noon the boys are all in, and as the catch is twice as numerous and twice as large as on the previous evening, and as the weather is all that could be asked of the longest days in June, they are in excellent spirits. The boxes are brought out, pork is sliced, a can of Indian meal comes to the front, and they go for the frying-pans.

"Holy Moses! Look here. Just see the ants and bugs."

Second Man.—"Well, I should say! I can see your ants and bugs, and go you an earwig better."

Third Man (inverting his pan spitefully over the fire).—"D—n 'em, I'll roast the beggars."

Bush D. (who is something of a cook and woodsman) "Boys, I'll take the pot. I've got a thousand-legged worm at the head of a pismire flush, and it serves us right, for a lot of slovens. Dishes should be cleaned as often as they are used. Now let's scour our pans and commence right."

Hot water, ashes, and soap soon restore the pans to pristine brightness; three frying-pans are filled with trout well rolled in meal; a fourth is used for cooking a can of tomatoes; the coffee is strong, and everything comes out without being smoked or scorched. The trout are browned to a turn, and even the O. W. admits that the dinner is a success. When it is over and the dishes are cleaned and put away, and the camp slicked up, there comes the usual two hours of lounging, smoking, and story telling, so dear to the hearts of those who love to go a-fishing and camping. At length there is a lull in the conversation, and Bush D. turns to the old woodsman with, "I thought, 'Uncle Mart,' you were going to show us fellows such a lot of kinks about camping out, camp-fires, cooking, and all that sort of thing, isn't it about time to begin? Strikes me you have spent most of the last twenty-four hours holding down that log."

"Except cutting some night wood and tending the fire," adds number two.

The old woodsman, who has been rather silent up to this time, knocks the ashes leisurely from his pipe, and gets on his feet for a few remarks. He says, "Boys, a bumblebee is biggest when it's first born. You've learned more than you think in the last twenty-four hours."

"Well, as how? Explain yourself," says Bush D.

O. W.—"In the first place, you have learned better than to stick your cooking-kit into a tumbled down heap of knots, mulch and wet bark, only to upset and melt down the pots, and scorch or smoke everything in the pans, until a starving hound wouldn't eat the mess. And you have found that it doesn't take a log heap to boil a pot of coffee or fry a pan of trout. Also, that a level bed of live coals makes an excellent cooking fire, though I will show you a better. Yesterday you cooked the worst meal I ever saw in the woods. Today you get up a really good, plain dinner; you have learned that much in one day. Oh, you improve some. And I think you have taken a lesson in cleanliness today."

"Yes; but we learned that of the ant—and bug," says number two.

O. W.—"Just so. And did you think all the ants and doodle-bugs blundered into that grease in one morning? I put 'em in myself—to give you a 'kink.' "

Bush D. (disgusted).—"You blasted, dirty old sinner."

Second Man.—"Oh, you miserable old swamp savage; I shan't get over that earwig in a month."

Third Man (plaintively).—"This life in the woods isn't what it's cracked up to be; I don't relish bugs and spiders. I wish I were home. I'm all bitten up with punkies, and——"

Fourth Man (savagely).—"Dashed old woods-loafer; let's tie his hands and fire him in the creek."

O. W. (placidly).—"Exactly, boys. Your remarks are terse, and to the point. Only, as I am going to show you a trick or two on woodcraft this afternoon, you can afford to wait a little. Now, quit smoking, and get out your hatchets; we'll go to work."

Three hatchets are brought to light; one of them a two-pound clumsy hand-axe, the others of an old time, Mt. Vernon, G. W. pattern. "And now," says good-natured Bush, "you give directions and we'll do the work."

G. W. Hatchet

Under directions, the coarse browse of the previous night is placed outside the shanty; three active youngsters, on hands and knees, feel out and cut off every offending stub and root inside the shanty, until it is smooth as a floor. The four small logs are brought to camp; the two longest are laid at the sides and staked in place; the others are placed, one at the head, the other at the foot, also staked; and the camp has acquired definite outlines, and a measurable size of eight by nine feet. Three hemlock logs and two sharpened stakes are toted to camp; the stakes driven firmly, and the logs laid against them, one above the other. Fire-dogs, forestick, etc., complete the arrangement, and the camp-fire is in shape for the coming night, precisely as shown in the engraving on page 33.

"And now," says the O. W., "if three of you will go down to the flat and pick the browse clean from the two hemlock tops, Bush and I will fix a cooking-range."

"A—what?" asks one.

"Going to start a boarding-house?" says another.

"Notion of going into the hardware business?" suggests a third.

"Never mind, sonny; just 'tend to that browse, and when you see a smoke raising on the flat by the spring, come over and see the range." And the boys, taking a couple of blankets in which to carry the browse, saunter away to the flat below.

A very leisurely aesthetic, fragrant occupation is this picking browse. It should never be cut, but pulled, stripped or broken. I have seen a Senator, ex-Governor, and a wealthy banker enjoying themselves hugely at it, varying the occupation by hacking small timber with their G. W. hatchets, like so many boys let loose from school. It may have looked a trifle undignified, but I dare say they found their account in it. Newport or Long Branch would have been more expensive, and much less healthful.

For an hour and a half tongues and fingers are busy around the hemlock tops; then a thin, long volume of blue smoke rises near the spring, and the boys walk over to inspect the range. They find it made as follows: Two logs six feet long and eight inches thick are laid parallel, but seven inches apart at one end and only four at the other. They are bedded firmly and flattened a little on the inside. On the upper sides the logs are carefully hewed and leveled until pots, pans and kettles will sit firmly and evenly on them. A strong forked stake is driven at each end of the space, and a cross-pole, two or three inches thick, laid on, for hanging kettles. This completes the range; simple, but effective. (See illustration.) The broad end of the space is for frying-pans, and the potato kettle. The narrow end, for coffee-pots and utensils of lesser diameter. From six to eight dishes can be cooked at the same time. Soups, stews, and beans are to be cooked in closely covered kettles hung from the cross-pole, the bottoms of the kettles reaching within some two inches of the logs. With a moderate fire they may be left to simmer for hours without care or attention.

The fire is of the first importance. Start it with fine kindling and clean, dry, hemlock bark. When you have a bright, even fire from end to end of the space, keep it up with small fagots of the sweetest and most wholesome woods in the forest. These are, in the order named, black birch, hickory, sugar maple, yellow birch, and red beech. The sticks should be short, and not over two inches across. Split wood is better than round. The out-door range can be made by one man in little more than an hour, and the camper-out, who once tries it, will never wish to see a "portable camp-stove" again.

When the sun leaves the valley in the shade of Asaph Mountain, the boys have a fragrant bed of elastic browse a foot deep in the shanty, with pillows improvised from stuffed boot legs, cotton handkerchiefs, etc. They cook their suppers on the range, and vote it perfect, no melting or heating handles too hot for use, and no smoking of dishes, or faces.

OUT-DOOR COOKING-RANGE

Just at dark—which means 9 P.M. in the last week of June—the fire is carefully made and chinked. An hour later it is throwing its grateful warmth and light directly into camp, and nowhere else. The camp turns in. Not to wriggle and quarrel with obdurate stubs, but to sleep. And sleep they do. The sound, deep, restful sleep of healthy young manhood, inhaling pure mountain air on the healthiest bed yet known to man.

When it is past midnight, and the fire burns low, and the chill night breeze drifts into camp, they still do not rouse up, but only spoon closer, and sleep right on. Only the O. W. turns out sleepily, at two bells in the middle watch, after the manner of hunters, trappers, and sailors, the world over. He quietly rebuilds the fire, reduces a bit of navy plug to its lowest denomination, and takes a solitary smoke—still holding down his favorite log. Quizzically and quietly he regards the sleeping youngsters, and wonders if among them all there is one who will do as he has done, i. e., relinquish all of what the world reckons as success, for the love of nature and a free forest life. He hopes not. And yet, as he glances at the calm yellow moon overhead, and listens to the low murmur of the little waterfall below the spring, he has a faint notion that it is not all loss and dross.

Knocking the ashes from his pipe he prepares to turn in, murmuring to himself, half sadly, half humorously, "I have been young, and now I am old; yet have I never seen the true woodsman forsaken, or his seed begging bread—or anything else, so to speak—unless it might be a little tobacco or a nip of whisky." And he creeps into his blanket-bag, backs softly out to the outside man, and joins the snorers.

It is broad daylight when he again turns out, leaving the rest still sleeping soundly. He starts a lively fire in the range, treats two coffee pots to a double handful of coffee and three pints of water each, sets on the potato kettle, washes the potatoes, then sticks his head into the camp, and rouses the party with a regular second mate's hail. "Star-a-ar-bo'lin's aho-o-o-y. Turn out, you beggars. Come on deck and see it rain." And the boys do turn out. Not with wakeful alacrity, but in a dazed, dreamy, sleepy way. They open wide eyes, when they see that the sun is turning the sombre tops of pines and hemlocks to a soft orange yellow.

"I'd have sworn," says one, "that I hadn't slept over fifteen minutes by the watch."

"And I," says another, "was just watching the fire, when I dropped off in a doze. In about five minutes I opened my eyes, and I'll be shot if it wasn't sunrise."

"As for me," says a third, "I don't know as I've slept at all. I remember seeing somebody poking the fire last night. Next thing I knew, some lunatic was yelling around camp about 'starbolin's,' and 'turning out.' Guess I'll lay down and have my nap out."

"Yes," says the O. W., "I would. If I was a healthy youngster, and couldn't get along with seven hours and a half of solid sleep, I'd take the next forenoon for it. Just at present, I want to remark that I've got the coffee and potato business underway, and I'll attend to them. If you want anything else for breakfast, you'll have to cook it."

And the boys, rising to the occasion, go about the breakfast with willing hands. It is noticeable, however, that only one pan of trout is cooked, two of the youngsters preferring to fall back on broiled ham, remarking that brook trout is too rich and cloying for a steady diet. Which is true. The appetite for trout has very sensibly subsided, and the boyish eagerness for trout fishing has fallen off immensely. Only two of the party show any interest in the riffles. They stroll down stream leisurely, to try their flies for an hour or two. The others elect to amuse themselves about the camp, cutting small timber with their little hatchets, picking fresh browse, or skirmishing the mountain side for wintergreen berries and sassafras. The fishermen return in a couple of hours, with a score of fair-sized trout. They remark apologetically that it is blazing hot—and there are plenty of trout ahead. Then they lean their rods against the shanty, and lounge on the blankets, and smoke and dose.

It is less than forty-eight hours since the cross-pole was laid; and, using a little common sense woodcraft, the camp has already attained to a systematic no-system of rest, freedom and idleness. Every man is free to "loaf, and invite his soul." There is good trouting within an hour's walk for those who choose, and there is some interest, with a little exercise, in cooking and cutting night wood, slicking up, etc. But the whole party is stricken with "camp-fever," "Indian laziness," the *dolce far niente*. It is over and around every man, enveloping him as with a roseate blanket from the Castle of Indolence.

It is the perfect summer camp.

And it is no myth; but a literal résumé of a five days' outing at Poplar Spring, on Marsh Creek, in Pennsylvania. Alas, for the beautiful valley, that once afforded the finest camping grounds I have ever known.

> Never any more
> Can it be
> Unto me (or anybody else)
> As before.

A huge tannery, six miles above Poplar Spring, poisons and

blackens the stream with chemicals, bark and ooze. The land has been brought into market, and every acre eagerly bought up by actual settlers. The once fine covers and thickets are converted into fields thickly dotted with blackened stumps. And, to crown the desolation, heavy laden trains of "The Pine Creek and Jersey Shore R. R." go thundering almost hourly over the very spot where stood our camp by Poplar Spring.

Of course, this is progress; but, whether backward or forward, had better be decided sixty years hence. And, just what has happened to the obscure valley of Marsh Creek, is happening today, on a larger scale, all over the land. It is the same old story of grab and greed. Let us go on the "make" today, and "whack up" tomorrow; cheating each other as villainously as we may, and posterity be d—d. "What's all the w-u-u-rld to a man when his wife is a widdy?"

This is the moral: From Maine to Montana; from the Adirondacks to Alaska; from the Yosemite to the Yellowstone, the trout-hog, the deer-wolf, the netter, the skin-hunter, each and all have it their own way; and the law is a farce—only to be enforced where the game has vanished forever. Perhaps the man-child is born who will live to write the moral of all this—when it is too late.

Chapter VII

MORE HINTS ON COOKING, WITH SOME SIMPLE RE-
CEIPTS—BREAD, COFFEE, POTATOES, SOUPS, STEWS,
BEANS, FISH, MEAT, VENISON

We may live without friends, we may live without books,
But civilized man cannot live without cooks.

IT is probably true that nothing connected with out-door life in camp is so badly botched as the cooking. It is not through any lack of the raw material, which may be had of excellent quality in any country village. It is not from lack of intelligence or education, for the men you meet in the woods, as outers or sportsmen, are rather over than under the average in these respects. Perhaps it is because it has been dinned into our ears from early childhood, that an appetite, a healthy longing for something good to eat, a tickling of the palate with wholesome, appetizing food, is beneath the attention of an aesthetic, intellectual man. Forgetting that the entire man, mental and physical, depends on proper aliment and the healthy assimilation thereof; and that a thin, dyspeptic man can no more keep up in the struggle of life, than the lightning express can make connections, drawn by a worn out locomotive.

I have never been able to get much help from cook-books, or the scores of recipes published in various works on out-door sport. Take, for example, Frank Forester's "Fish and Fishing." He has more than seventy recipes for cooking fish, over forty of which contain terms or names in French. I dare say they are good—for a first-class hotel. I neither cook nor converse in French, and I have come to know that the plainest cooking is the best, so that it be well done and wholesome. In making up the rations for camping out, the first thing usually attended to is bread. And if this be light, well-made bread, enough may be taken along to last four or five days, and this may be eked out with Boston crackers, or the best hard-tack, for a couple or three days more, without the least hardship. Also, there are few camps in which some one is not going out to the clearings every few days for mail, small stores, etc., and a supply of bread can be arranged for, with less trouble than it can be made. There are times, however, when this is not feasible, and there are men who prefer warm bread all the time. In this case the usual resort, from Maine to Alaska, is the universal flapjack. I do not like it; I seldom make it; it is not good. But it may be eaten, with maple syrup or sugar and butter. I prefer a plain water Johnnycake, made as follows (supposing your tins are something like those described in Chapter II): Put a little more than a pint of water in your kettle and bring it to a sharp boil, adding a small teaspoonful of salt, and two of sugar. Stir in slowly enough good corn meal to make a rather stiff mush, let it cook a few minutes, and set it off the fire; then grease your largest tin dish and put the mush in it, smoothing it on top. Set the dish on the out-door range described in the previous chapter, with a lively bed of coal beneath—but no blaze. Invert the second sized tin over the cake, and cover the dish with bright live coals, that bottom and top may bake evenly, and give it from thirty-five to forty minutes for baking. It makes wholesome, palatable bread, which gains on the taste with use.

Those who prefer wheat bread can make a passable article by using the best wheat flour with baking powders, mixing three tablespoonfuls of the powders to a quart of flour. Mix and knead thoroughly with warm water to a rather thin dough, and bake as above. Use the same proportions for pancake batter. When stopping in a permanent camp with plenty of time to cook, excellent light bread may be made by using dry yeast cakes, though it is not necessary to "set" the sponge as directed on the papers. Scrape and dissolve half a cake of the yeast in a gill of warm water, and mix it with the flour. Add warm water enough to make it pliable, and not too stiff; set in a warm place until it rises sufficiently, and bake as directed above. It takes several hours to rise.

I am afraid I shall discount my credit on camp cooking when I admit that—if I must use fine flour—I prefer unleavened bread; what my friends irreverently call "club bread." Not that it was ever made or endorsed by any club of men that I know of, but because it is baked on a veritable club, sassafras or black birch. This is how to make it: Cut a club two feet long and three inches thick at the broadest end; peel or shave off the bark smoothly, and sharpen the smaller end neatly. Then stick the sharpened end in the ground near the fire, leaning the broad end toward a bed of live coals, where it will get screeching hot. While it is heating, mix rather more than a half pint of best Minnesota flour with enough warm water to make a dough. Add a half teaspoonful of salt, and a teaspoonful of sugar, and mould and pull the dough until it becomes lively. Now, work it into a ribbon two inches wide and half an inch thick, wind the ribbon spirally around the broad end of the club, stick the latter in front of the fire so that the bread will bake evenly and quickly to a light brown, and turn frequently until done, which will be in about thirty minutes. When done take it from the fire, stand the club firmly upright, and pick the bread off in pieces as you want it to eat. It will keep hot a long time, and one soon becomes fond of it.

To make perfect coffee, just two ingredients are necessary, and only two. These are water and coffee. It is owing to the bad management of the latter that we drink poor coffee.

Mocha is generally considered to be the best type of coffee, with Java a close second. It is the fashion at present to mix the two in proportions to suit, some taking two parts Java to one of Mocha, others reversing these proportions. Either way is good, or the Mocha is quite as good alone. But there is a better berry than either for the genuine coffee toper. This is the small, dark green berry that comes to market under the generic name of Rio, that name covering half a dozen grades of coffee raised in different provinces of Brazil, throughout a country extending north and south for more than 1,200 miles. The berry alluded to is produced along the range of high hills to the westward of Bahia, and extending north toward the Parnahiba. It has never arrested attention as a distinct grade of the article, but it contains more coffee or caffein to the pound than any berry known to commerce. It is the smallest, heaviest and darkest green of any coffee that comes to our market from Brazil, and may be known by these traits. I have tested it in the land where it is grown, and also at home, for the past sixteen years, and I place it at the head of the list, with Mocha next. Either will make perfect coffee, if treated as follows: Of the berry, browned and ground, take six heaping tablespoonfuls, and add three pints of cold water; place the kettle over the fire and bring to a sharp boil; set it a little aside where it will bubble and simmer until wanted, and just before pouring, drip in a half gill of cold water to settle it. That is all there is to it. The quantity of berry is about twice as much as usually given in recipes; but if you want coffee, you had better add two spoonfuls than cut off one.

In 1867, and again in 1870, I had occasion to visit the West India Islands and Brazil. In common with most coffee topers, I had heard much of the super-excellence ascribed to "West India coffee" and "Brazilian coffee." I concluded to investigate. I had rooms at the Hotel d'Europe, Para, North Brazil. There were six of us, English and American boarders. Every morning, before we were out of our hammocks, a barefooted, half naked Mina negress came around and served each of us with a small cup of strong, black coffee, and sugar ad libitum. There was not enough of it for a drink; it was rather in the nature of a medicine, and so intended—"To kill the biscos," they said. The coffee was above criticism.

I went, in the dark of a tropical morning, with Senhor João, to the coffee factory where they browned the berry, and saw him buy a pound, smoking hot, for which he paid twenty-five cents, or quite as much as it would cost in New York. In ten minutes the coffee was at the hotel, and ground. This is the way they brewed it: A round-bottomed kettle was sitting on the brick range, with a half gallon of boiling water in it. Over the kettle a square piece of white flannel was suspended, caught up at the corners like a dip net. In this the coffee was placed, and a small darky put in his time steadily with a soup ladle, dipping the boiling water from the kettle and pouring it on the coffee. There was a constant stream percolating through coffee and cloth, which, in the course of half an hour, became almost black, and clear as brandy. This was "Brazilian coffee." As the cups used were very small, and as none but the Northerners drank more than one cup, I found that the hotel did not use over two quarts of coffee each morning. It struck me that a pound of fresh Rio coffee berry ought to make a half gallon of rather powerful coffee.

On my arrival home—not having any small darky or any convenient arrangement for the dip net—I had a sack made of light, white flannel, holding about one pint. In this I put one-quarter pound of freshly ground berry, with water enough for five large cups. It was boiled thoroughly, and proved just as good as the Brazilian article, but too strong for any of the family except the writer. Those who have a fancy for clear, strong "Brazilian coffee," will see how easily and simply it can be made.

But, on a heavy knapsack-and-rifle tramp among the mountains, or a lone canoe cruise in a strange wilderness, I do not carry coffee. I prefer tea. Often, when too utterly tired and beaten for further travel, I have tried coffee, whisky or brandy, and a long experience convinces me that there is nothing so restful and refreshing to an exhausted man as a dish of strong, green tea. To make it as it should be made, bring the water to a high boil, and let it continue to boil for a full minute. Set it off the fire and it will cease boiling; put in a handful of tea, and it will instantly boil up again; then set it near the fire, where it will simmer for a few minutes, when it will be ready for use. Buy the best green tea you can find, and use it freely on a hard tramp. Black, or Oolong tea, is excellent in camp. It should be put in the pot with cold water and brought to the boiling point.

Almost any man can cook potatoes, but few cook them well. Most people think them best boiled in their jackets, and to cook them perfectly in this manner is so simple and easy, that the wonder is how any one can fail. A kettle of screeching hot water with a small handful of salt in it, good potatoes of nearly equal size, washed clean and clipped at the ends, these are the requisites. Put the potatoes in the boiling water, cover closely, and keep the water at high boiling pitch until you can thrust a sharp sliver through the largest potato. Then drain off the water, and set the kettle in a hot place with the lid partly off. Take them out only as they are wanted; lukewarm potatoes are not good. They will be found about as good as potatoes can be, when cooked in their jackets. But there is a better way, as thus: Select enough for a mess, of smooth, sound tubers; pare them carefully, taking off as little as possible, because the best of the potato lies nearest the skin, and cook as above. When done, pour the water off to the last drop; sprinkle a spoonful of salt and fine cracker crumbs over them; then shake, roll, and rattle them in the kettle until the outsides are white and floury. Keep them piping hot until wanted. It is the way to have perfect boiled potatoes.

Many outers are fond of roast potatoes in camp; and they mostly spoil them in the roasting, although there is no better place than the camp-fire in which to do it. To cook them aright, scoop out a basinlike depression under the fore-stick, three or four inches deep, and large enough to hold the tubers when laid side by side; fill it with bright, hard-wood coals, and keep up a strong heat for half an hour or more. Next, clean out the hollow, place the potatoes in it, and cover them with hot sand or ashes, topped with a heap of glowing coals, and keep up all the heat you like. In about forty minutes commence to try them with a sharpened hard-wood sliver; when this will pass through them they are done, and should be raked out at once. Run the sliver through them from end to end, to let the steam escape, and use immediately, as a roast potato quickly becomes soggy and bitter. I will add that, in selecting a supply of potatoes for camp, only the finest and smoothest should be taken.

A man may be a trout-crank, he may have been looking forward for ten weary months to the time when he is to strike the much dreamed of mountain stream, where trout may be taken and eaten without stint. Occasionally—not often—his dream is realized. For two or three days he revels in fly-fishing, and eating brook trout. Then his enthusiasm begins to subside. He talks less of his favorite flies, and hints that wading hour after hour in ice-water gives him cramps in the calves of his legs. Also, he finds that brook trout, eaten for days in succession, pall on the appetite. He hankers for the flesh-pots of the restaurant, and his soul yearns for the bean-pot of home.

Luckily, some one has brought a sack of white beans, and the expert—there is always an expert in camp—is deputed to cook them. He accepts the trust, and proceeds to do it. He puts a quart of dry beans and a liberal chunk of pork in a two-quart kettle, covers the mess with water, and brings it to a rapid boil. Presently the beans begin to swell and lift the lid of the kettle; their conduct is simply demoniacal. They lift up the lid of the kettle, they tumble out over the rim in a way to provoke a saint, and they have scarcely begun to cook. The expert is not to be beaten. As they rise, he spoons them out and throws them away, until half of the best beans being wasted, the rest settle to business. He fills the kettle with water and watches it for an hour. When bean-skins and scum arise he uses the spoon; and when a ring of greasy salt forms around the rim of the kettle, he carefully scrapes it off, but most of it drops back into the pot. When the beans seem cooked to the point of disintegration, he lifts off the kettle, and announces dinner. It is not a success. The largest beans are granulated rather than cooked, while the mealy portion of them has fallen to the bottom of the kettle, and become scorched thereon, and the smaller beans are too hard to be eatable. The liquid, that should be palatable bean soup, is greasy salt water, and the pork is half raw. The party falls back, hungry and disgusted. Even if the mess were well cooked, it is too salt for eating. And why should this be so? Why should any sensible man spend years in acquiring an education that shall fit him for the struggle of life, yet refuse to spend a single day in learning how to cook the food that must sustain the life? It is one of the conundrums no one will ever find out.

There is no article of food more easily carried, and none that contains more nourishment to the pound, than the bean. Limas are usually preferred, but the large white marrow is just as good. It will pay to select them carefully. Keep an eye on grocery stocks, and when you strike a lot of extra large, clean beans, buy twice as many as you need for camp use. Spread them on a table, a quart at a time, and separate the largest and best from the others. Fully one-half will go to the side of the largest and finest, and these may be put in a muslin bag, and kept till wanted. Select the expeditionary pork with equal care, buying nothing but thick, solid, "clear," with a pink tinge. Reject that which is white and lardy. With such material, if you cannot lay over Boston baked beans, you had better sweep the cook out of camp.

This is how to cook them: Put a pound or a little more of clean pork in the kettle, with water enough to cover it. Let it boil slowly half an hour. In the meantime, wash and parboil one pint of beans. Drain the water from the pork and place the beans around it; add two quarts of water and hang the kettle where it will boil steadily, but not rapidly, for two hours. Pare neatly and thinly five or six medium sized potatoes, and allow them from thirty to forty minutes (according to size and variety), in which to cook. They must be pressed down among the beans so as to be entirely covered. If the beans be fresh and fine they will probably fall to pieces before time is up. This, if they are not allowed to scorch, makes them all the better. If a portion of pork be left over, it is excellent sliced very thin when cold, and eaten with bread. The above is a dinner for three or four hungry men.

It is usually the case that some of the party prefer baked beans. To have these in perfection, add one gill of raw beans and a piece of pork three inches square to the foregoing proportions. Boil as above, until the beans begin to crack open; then fork out the smaller piece of pork, place it in the center of your largest cooking tin, take beans enough from the kettle to nearly fill the tin, set it over a bright fire on the range, invert the second sized tin for a cover, place live, hard-wood coals on top, and bake precisely as directed for bread—only, when the coals on top become dull and black, brush them off, raise the cover, and take a look. If the beans are getting too dry, add three or four spoonfuls of liquor from the kettle, replace cover and coals, and let them bake until they are of a rich light brown on top. Then serve. It is a good dish. If Boston can beat it, I don't want to lay up anything for old age.

Brown bread and baked beans have a natural connection in the average American mind, and rightly. They supplement each other, even as spring lamb and green peas with our transatlantic cousins. But there is a better recipe for brown bread than is known to the dwellers of the Hub—one that has captured first prizes at country fairs, and won the approval of epicures from Maine to Minnesota; the one that brought honest old Greeley down, on his strictures anent "country bread." And here is the recipe; take it for what it is worth, and try it fairly before condemning it. It is for home use: One quart of sweet milk, one quart of sour, two quarts of Indian meal and one quart of flour, and a cupful of dark, thin Porto Rico molasses. Use one teaspoonful of soda only. Bake in a steady, moderate oven, for four hours. Knead thoroughly before baking.

Soup is, or should be, a leading food element in every woodland camp. I am sorry to say that nothing is, as a rule, more badly botched, while nothing is more easily or simply cooked as it should be. Soup requires time, and a solid basis of the right material. Venison is the basis, and the best material is the bloody part of the deer, where the bullet went through. We used to throw this away; we have learned better. Cut about four pounds of the bloody meat into convenient pieces, and wipe them as clean as possible with leaves or a damp cloth, but don't wash them. Put the meat into a five-quart kettle nearly filled with water, and raise it to a lively boiling pitch. Let it boil for two hours. Have ready a three-tined fork made from a branch of birch or beech, and with this test the meat from time to time; when it parts readily from the bones, slice in a large onion. Pare six large, smooth potatoes, cut five of them into quarters, and drop them into the kettle; scrape the sixth one into the soup for thickening. Season with salt and white pepper to taste.

When, by skirmishing with the wooden fork, you can fish up bones with no meat on them, the soup is cooked, and the kettle may be set aside to cool. Any hungry sportsman can order the next motion. Squirrels—red, black, gray or fox—make nearly as good a soup as venison, and better stew. Hares, rabbits, grouse, quail, or any of the smaller game birds, may be used in making soup; but all small game is better in a stew.

To make a stew, proceed for the first two hours precisely as directed for soup; then slice in a couple of good-sized onions and six medium potatoes. When the meat begins to fall from the bones, make a thickening by rubbing three tablespoonfuls of flour and two spoonfuls of melted butter together; thin to the consistency of cream with liquor from the kettle, and drip slowly into the stew, stirring briskly meanwhile. Allow all soups and stews to boil two hours before seasoning, and use only the best table salt and white (or black) pepper. Season sparingly; it is easier to put salt in than to get it out. Cayenne pepper adds zest to a soup or stew, but, as some dislike it, let each man season his plate to his own cheek.

Fried squirrels are excellent for a change, but are mostly spoiled by poor cooks, who put tough old he's and tender young squirrels together, treating all alike. To dress and cook them properly, chop off heads, tails and feet with the hatchet; cut the skin on the back crosswise, and, inserting the two middle fingers, pull the skin off in two parts, (head and tail). Clean and cut them in halves, leaving two ribs on the hindquarters. Put hind and fore quarters into the kettle, and parboil until tender. This will take about twenty minutes for young ones, and twice as long for the old.

When a sharpened sliver will pass easily through the flesh, take the hindquarters from the kettle, drain, and place them in the frying-pan with pork fat hissing hot. Fry to a light, rich brown. It is the only proper way to cook squirrels. The forequarters are to be left in the kettle for a stew.

It sometimes happens that pigeons are very plentiful, and the camp is tempted into over-shooting and over-cooking, until every one is thoroughly sick of pigeons. This is all wrong. No party is, or can be, justified in wanton slaughter, just because birds happen to be plentiful; they will soon be scarce enough. Pigeons are hardly game, and they are not a first-class bird; but a good deal may be got out of them by the following method: Dress them, at the rate of two birds to one man; save the giblets; place in the kettle, and boil until the sliver will easily pierce the breast; fork them out, cut the thick meat from each side of the breast bone, roll slightly in flour, and put the pieces in the pan, frying them in the same way as directed for squirrels. Put the remainder of the birds in the kettle for a stew.

Quail are good cooked in the same manner, but are better roasted or broiled. To roast them, parboil for fifteen minutes, and in the meantime cut a thin hard-wood stick, eighteen inches long for each bird. Sharpen the sticks neatly at both ends; impale the birds on one end and thrust the sticks into the ground near the fire, leaning them so that the heat will strike strongly and evenly. Hang a strip of pork between the legs of each bird, and turn frequently until they are a rich brown. When the sharpened sliver will pass easily through the breast they are done.

Woodcock are to be plucked, but not drawn. Suspend the bird in a bright, clear heat, hang a ribbon of fat pork between the legs, and roast until well done; do not parboil him.

Ruffed grouse are excellent roasted in the same manner, but should first be parboiled. Mallards, teal, butterballs, all edible ducks, are to be treated the same as grouse. If you are ever lucky enough to feast on a canvas-back roasted as above, you will be apt to borrow a leaf from Oliver Twist.

Venison steak should be pounded to tenderness, pressed and worked into shape with the hunting-knife, and broiled over a bed of clean hard-wood coals. A three-pronged birch fork makes the best broiler. For roast venison, the best portion is the forward part of the saddle. Trim off the flanky parts and ends of the ribs; split the backbone lengthwise, that the inner surface may be well exposed; hang it by a strong cord or bark string in a powerful, even heat; lay thin strips of pork along the upper edge, and turn from time to time until done. It had better be left a little rare than overdone. Next to the saddle for roasting, comes the shoulder. Peel this smoothly from the side, using the hunting knife; trim neatly, and cut off the leg at the knee; gash the thickest part of the flesh, and press shreds of pork into the gashes, with two or three thin slices skewered to the upper part. Treat it in the roasting as described above. It is not equal to the saddle when warm, but sliced and eaten cold, is quite as good.

And do not despise the fretful porcupine; he is better than he looks. If you happen on a healthy young specimen when you are needing meat, give him a show before condemning him. Shoot him humanely in the head, and dress him. It is easily done; there are no quills on the belly, and the skin peels as freely as a rabbit's. Take him to camp, parboil him for thirty minutes, and roast or broil him to a rich brown over a bed of glowing coals. He will need no pork to make him juicy, and you will find him very like spring lamb, only better.

I do not accept the decision that ranks the little gray rabbit as a hare, simply because he has a slit in his lip; at all events I shall call him a rabbit for convenience, to distinguish him from his long-legged cousin, who turns white in winter, never takes to a hole, and can keep ahead of hounds nearly all day, affording a game, musical chase that is seldom out of hearing. He never by any chance has an ounce of fat on him, and is not very good eating. He can, however, be worked into a good stew or a passable soup—provided he has not been feeding on laurel. The rabbit is an animal of different habits, and different attributes. When jumped from his form, he is apt to "dig out" for a hole or the nearest stone heap. Sometimes an old one will potter around a thicket, ahead of a slow dog, but his tendency is always to hole. But he affords some sport, and as an article of food, beats the long-legged hare out of sight. He is excellent in stews or soups, while the after half of him, flattened down with the hatchet, parboiled and fried brown in butter or pork fat, is equal to spring chicken.

In the cooking of fish, as of flesh and fowl, the plainest and simplest methods are best; and for anything under two pounds, it is not necessary to go beyond the frying-pan. Trout of over a pound should be split down the back, that they may lie well in the pan, and cook evenly. Roll well in meal, or a mixture of meal and flour, and fry to a rich brown in pork fat, piping hot. Larger fish may just as well be fried, but are also adapted to other methods, and there are people who like fish broiled and buttered, or boiled. To broil a fish, split him on the back and broil him four minutes, flesh side down, turn and broil the other side an equal time. Butter and season to taste. To broil, the fish should weigh three pounds or more. Clean, and crimp him by gashing the sides deeply with a sharp knife. Put him in a kettle of boiling water strongly salted, and boil twenty-five minutes. For each additional pound above three, add five minutes. For gravy, rub together two tablespoonfuls of flour and one of melted butter, add one heaping teaspoonful of evaporated milk, and thin with liquor from the kettle. When done, it should have the consistency of cream. Take the fish from the kettle, drain, pour the gravy over it, and eat only with wheat bread or hard-tack, with butter. The simplest is best, healthiest, and most appetizing.

As a rule, on a mountain tramp or a canoe cruise, I do not tote canned goods. I carry my duffle in a light, pliable knapsack, and there is an aggravating antagonism between the uncompromising rims of a fruit-can, and the knobs of my vertebrae, that twenty years of practice have utterly failed to reconcile. And yet, I have found my account in a can of condensed milk, not for tea or coffee, but on bread as a substitute for butter. And I have found a small can of Boston baked beans a most helpful lunch, with a nine-mile carry ahead. It was not epicurean, but had staying qualities.

I often have a call to pilot some muscular young friend into the deep forest, and he usually carries a large pack-basket, with a full supply of quart cans of salmon, tomatoes, peaches, etc. As in duty bound, I admonish him kindly, but firmly, on the folly of loading his young shoulders with such effeminate luxuries; often, I fear, hurting his young feelings by brusque advice. But at night, when the camp-fire burns brightly, and he begins to fish out his tins, the heart of the Old Woodsman relents, and I make amends by allowing him to divide the groceries.

There is a method of cooking usually called "mudding up," which I have found to preserve the flavor and juiciness of ducks, grouse, etc., better than any other method. I described the method in *Forest and Stream* more than a year ago, but a brief repetition may not be out of place here. Suppose the bird to be cooked is a mallard, or better still, a canvas-back. Cut off the head and most part of the neck; cut off the pinions and pull out the tail feathers, make a plastic cake of clay or tenacious earth an inch thick, and large enough to envelop the bird, and cover him with it snugly. Dig an oval pit under the fore-stick, large enough to hold him, and fill it with hot coals, keeping up a strong heat. Just before turning in for the night, clean out the pit, put in the bird, cover with hot embers and coals, keeping up a brisk fire over it all night. When taken out in the morning you will have an oval, oblong mass of baked clay, with a well roasted bird inside. Let the mass cool until it can be handled, break off the clay, and feathers and skin will come with it, leaving the bird clean and skinless. Season it as you eat, with salt, pepper, and a squeeze of lemon if you like, nothing else.

In selecting salt, choose that which has a gritty feel when rubbed between the thumb and finger, and use white pepper rather than black, grinding the berry yourself. Procure a common tin pepper-box, and fill it with a mixture of fine salt and Cayenne pepper—ten spoonsfuls of the former and one of the latter. Have it always where you can lay your hand on it; you will come to use it daily in camp, and if you ever get lost, you will find it of value. Fish and game have a flat, flashy taste eaten without salt, and are also unwholesome.

Do not carry any of the one hundred and one condiments, sauces, garnishes, etc., laid down in the books. Salt, pepper, and lemons fill the bill in that line. Lobster-sauce, shrimp-sauce, marjoram, celery, parsley, thyme, anchovies, etc., may be left at the hotels.

It may be expected that a pocket volume on woodcraft should contain a liberal chapter of instruction on hunting. It would be quite useless. Hunters, like poets, are born, not made. The art cannot be taught on paper. A few simple hints, however, may not be misplaced. To start aright, have your clothes fitted for hunting. Select good cassimere of a sort of dull, no-colored, neutral tint, like a decayed stump, and have coat, pants, and cap made of it. For foot-gear, two pairs of heavy yarn socks, with rubber shoes or buckskin moccasins. In hunting, "silence is gold." Go quietly, slowly, and silently. Remember that the bright-eyed, sharp-eared woodfolk can see, hear and smell, with a keenness that throws your dull faculties quite in the shade. As you go lumbering and stick-breaking through the woods, you will never know how many of these quietly leave your path to right and left, allowing you to pass, while they glide away, unseen, unknown. It is easily seen that a sharp-sensed, light-bodied denizen of the woods can detect the approach of a heavy, bifurcated, booted animal, a long way ahead, and avoid him accordingly.

But there is an art, little known and practiced, that invariably succeeds in outflanking most wild animals; an art, simple in conception and execution, but requiring patience; a species, so to speak, of high art in forestry—the art of "sitting on a log." I could enlarge on this. I might say that the only writer of any note who has mentioned this phase of woodcraft is Mr. Charles D. Warner; and he only speaks of it in painting the character of that lazy old guide, "Old Phelps."

Sitting on a log includes a deal of patience, with oftentimes cold feet and chattering teeth; but, attended to faithfully and patiently, is quite as successful as chasing a deer all day on tracking snow, while it can be practiced when the leaves are dry, and no other mode of still-hunting offers the ghost of a chance. When a man is moving through the woods, wary, watchful animals are pretty certain to catch sight of him. But let him keep perfectly quiet and the conditions are reversed. I have had my best luck, and killed my best deer, by practically waiting hour after hour on runways. But the time when a hunter could get four or five fair shots in a day by watching a runway has passed away forever. Never any more will buffalo be seen in solid masses covering square miles in one pack. The immense bands of elk and droves of deer are things of the past, and "The game must go."

Chapter VIII

A TEN DAYS' TRIP IN THE WILDERNESS—GOING IT
ALONE

BOUT the only inducements I can think of for making a ten days' journey through a strong wilderness, solitary and alone, were a liking for adventure, intense love of nature in her wildest dress, and a strange fondness for being in deep forests by myself. The choice of route was determined by the fact that two old friends and schoolmates had chosen to cast their lots in Michigan, one near Saginaw Bay, the other among the pines of the Muskegon. And both were a little homesick, and both wrote frequent letters, in which, knowing my weak point, they exhausted their adjectives and adverbs in describing the abundance of game and the marvelous fishing. Now, the Muskegon friend—Davis—was pretty well out of reach. But Pete Williams, only a few miles out of Saginaw, was easily accessible. And so it happened, on a bright October morning, when there came a frost that cut from Maine to Missouri, that a sudden fancy took me to use my new Billinghurst on something larger than squirrels. It took about one minute to decide, and an hour to pack such duffle as I needed for a few weeks in the woods.

Remembering Pete's two brown-eyed "kids," and knowing that they were ague-stricken and homesick, I made place for a few apples and peaches, with a ripe melon. For Pete and I had been chums in Rochester, and I had bunked in his attic on Galusha Street, for two years. Also, his babies thought as much of me as of their father. The trip to Saginaw was easy and pleasant. A "Redbird" packet to Buffalo, the old propeller

Globe to Lower Saginaw, and a ride of half a day on a buck-board, brought me to Pete Williams' clearing. Were they glad to see me? Well, I think so. Pete and his wife cried like children, while the two little homesick "kids" laid their silken heads on my knees and sobbed for very joy. When I brought out the apples and peaches, assuring them that these came from the little garden of their old home—liar that I was—their delight was boundless. And the fact that their favorite tree was a "sour bough," while these were sweet, did not shake their faith in the least.

I stayed ten days or more with the Williams family, and the fishing and hunting were all that he had said—all that could be asked. The woods swarmed with pigeons and squirrels; grouse, quail, ducks and wild turkeys were too plentiful, while a good hunter could scarcely fail of getting a standing shot at a deer in a morning's hunt. But, *cui bono?* What use could be made of fish or game in such a place? They were all half sick, and had little appetite. Mrs. Williams could not endure the smell of fish; they had been cloyed on small game, and were surfeited on venison.

My sporting ardor sank to zero. I had the decency not to slaughter game for the love of killing, and leave it to rot, or hook large fish that could not be used. I soon grew restless, and began to think often about the lumber camp on the Muskegon. By surveyors' lines it was hardly more than sixty miles from Pete Williams' clearing to the Joe Davis camp on the Muskegon. "But practically," said Pete, "Joe and I are a thousand miles apart. White men, as a rule, don't undertake to cross this wilderness. The only one I know who has tried it is old Bill Hance; he can tell you all about it."

Hance was the hunting and trapping genius of Saginaw Bay —a man who dwelt in the woods summer and winter, and never trimmed his hair or wore any other covering on his head. Not a misanthrope, or taciturn, but friendly and talkative rather; liking best to live alone, but fond of tramping across the woods to gossip with neighbors; a very tall man withal, and so thin that, as he went rapidly winding and turning among fallen logs, you looked to see him tangle up and tumble in a loose coil, like a wet rope, but he was better than he looked. He

had a high reputation as trailer, guide, or trapper, and was
mentioned as a "bad man in a racket." I had met him several
times, and as he was decidedly a character, had rather laid myself out to cultivate him. And now that I began to have a
strong notion of crossing the woods alone, I took counsel of
Bill Hance. Unlike Williams, he thought it perfectly feasible,
and rather a neat, gamy thing for a youngster to do. He had
crossed the woods several times with surveying parties, and
once alone. He knew an Indian trail which led to an old camp
within ten miles of the Muskegon, and thought the trail could
be followed. It took him a little less than three days to go
through; "but," he added, "I nat'rally travel a little faster in
the woods than most men. If you can follow the trail, you
ought to get through in a little more'n three days—if you keep
moggin'."

One afternoon I carefully packed the knapsack and organized
for a long woods tramp. I took little stock in that trail, or the
three days' notion as to time. I made calculations on losing the
trail the first day, and being out a full week. The outfit consisted of rifle, hatchet, compass, blanket-bag, knapsack and knife.
For rations, one loaf of bread, two quarts of meal, two pounds
of pork, one pound of sugar, with tea, salt, etc., and a supply
of jerked venison. One tin dish, twelve rounds of ammunition,
and the bullet-molds, filled the list, and did not make a heavy
load.

Early on a crisp, bright October morning I kissed the little
fellows good-bye, and started out with Hance, who was to put
me on the trail. I left the children with sorrow and pity at
heart. I am glad now that my visit was a golden hiatus in the
sick monotony of their young lives, and that I was able to
brighten a few days of their dreary existence. They had begged
for the privilege of sleeping with me on a shake-down from
the first; and when, as often happened, a pair of little feverish
lips would murmur timidly and pleadingly, "I'm so dry; can I
have er drink?" I am thankful that I did not put the pleader
off with a sip of tepid water, but always brought it from the
spring, sparkling and cold. For, a twelvemonth later, there were
two little graves in a corner of the stump-blackened garden, and
two sore hearts in Pete Williams' cabin.

Hance found the trail easily, but the Indians had been gone a long time, and it was filled with leaves, dim, and not easy to follow. It ended as nearly all trails do; it branched off to right and left, grew dimmer and slimmer, degenerated to a deer path, petered out to a squirrel track, ran up a tree, and ended in a knot hole. I was not sorry. It left me free to follow my nose, my inclination, and—the compass.

There are men who, on finding themselves alone in a pathless forest, become appalled, almost panic stricken. The vastness of an unbroken wilderness subdues them, and they quail before the relentless, untamed forces of nature. These are the men who grow enthusiastic—at home—about sylvan life, outdoor sports, but always strike camp and come home rather sooner than they intended. And there be some who plunge into an unbroken forest with a feeling of fresh, free, invigorating delight, as they might dash into a crisp ocean surf on a hot day. These know that nature is stern, hard, immovable and terrible in unrelenting cruelty. When wintry winds are out and the mercury far below zero, she will allow her most ardent lover to freeze on her snowy breast without waving a leaf in pity, or offering him a match; and scores of her devotees may starve to death in as many different languages before she will offer a loaf of bread. She does not deal in matches and loaves; rather in thunderbolts and granite mountains. And the ashes of her camp-fires bury proud cities. But, like all tyrants, she yields to force, and gives the more, the more she is beaten. She may starve or freeze the poet, the scholar, the scientist; all the same, she has in store food, fuel and shelter, which the skillful, self-reliant woodsman can wring from her savage hand with axe and rifle.

> Only to him whose coat of rags
>   Has pressed at night her regal feet,
>   Shall come the secrets, strange and sweet,
> Of century pines and beetling crags.
>
> For him the goddess shall unlock
>   The golden secrets which have lain
>   Ten thousand years, through frost and rain,
> Deep in the bosom of the rock.

The trip was a long and tiresome one, considering the distance. There were no hairbreadth escapes; I was not tackled by bears, treed by wolves, or nearly killed by a hand-to-claw "racket" with a panther; and there were no Indians to come sneak-hunting around after hair. Animal life was abundant, exuberant, even. But the bright-eyed woodfolk seemed tame, nay, almost friendly, and quite intent on minding their own business. It was a "pigeon year," a "squirrel year," and also a marvelous year for shack, or mast. Every nut-bearing tree was loaded with sweet well-filled nuts; and this, coupled with the fact that the Indians had left, and the whites had not yet got in, probably accounted for the plentitude of game.

I do not think there was an hour of daylight on the trip when squirrels were not too numerous to be counted, while pigeons were a constant quantity from start to finish. Grouse in the thickets, and quail in the high oak openings, or small prairies, with droves of wild turkeys among heavy timber, were met with almost hourly, and there was scarcely a day on which I could not have had a standing shot at a bear. But the most interesting point about the game was—to me, at least—the marvelous abundance of deer. They were everywhere, on all sorts of ground and among all varieties of timber; very tame they were, too, often stopping to look at the stranger, offering easy shots at short range, and finally going off quite leisurely.

No ardent lover of forest life could be lonely in such company, and in such weather. The only drawback was the harassing and vexatious manner in which lakes, streams, swamps and marshes constantly persisted in getting across the way, compelling long detours to the north or south, when the true course was nearly due west. I think there were days on which ten hours of pretty faithful tramping did not result in more than three or four miles of direct headway. The headwaters of the Salt and Chippewa rivers were especially obstructive; and, when more than half the distance was covered, I ran into a tangle of small lakes, marshes and swamps, not marked on the map, which cost a hard day's work to leave behind.

While there were no startling adventures, and no danger connected with the trip, there was a constant succession of incidents, that made the lonely tramp far from monotonous. Some of these occurrences were intensely interesting, and a little exciting. Perhaps the brief recital of a few may not be uninteresting at the present day, when game is so rapidly disappearing.

My rifle was a neat, hair-triggered Billinghurst, carrying sixty round balls to the pound, a muzzle-loader, of course, and a nail-driver. I made just three shots in ten days, and each shot stood for a plump young deer in the "short blue." It seemed wicked to murder such a bright, graceful animal, when no more than the loins and a couple of slices from the ham could be used, leaving the balance to the wolves, who never failed to take possession before I was out of ear shot. But I condoned the excess, if excess it were, by the many chances I allowed to pass, not only on deer but bear, and once on a big brute of a wild hog, the wickedest and most formidable looking animal I ever met in the woods. The meeting happened in this wise. I had been bothered and wearied for half a day by a bad piece of low, marshy ground, and had at length struck a dry, rolling oak opening where I sat down at the foot of a small oak to rest. I had scarcely been resting ten minutes, when I caught sight of a large, dirty-white animal, slowly working its way in my direction through the low bushes, evidently nosing around for acorns. I was puzzled to say what it was. It looked like a hog, but stood too high on its legs; and how would such a beast get there anyhow? Nearer and nearer he came, and at last walked out into an open spot less than twenty yards distant. It was a wild hog of the ugliest and largest description; tall as a yearling, with an unnaturally large head, and dangerous looking tusks, that curved above his savage snout like small horns. There was promise of magnificent power in his immense shoulders, while flanks and hams were disproportionately light. He came out to the open leisurely munching his acorns, or amusing himself by ploughing deep furrows with his nose, and not until within ten yards did he appear to note the presence of a stranger. Suddenly he raised his head and became rigid as though frozen to stone; he was taking an observation. For a few seconds he remained immovable, then his bristles became erect, and with a deep guttural, grunting noise, he commenced hitching himself along in my direction, sidewise. My hair raised, and in an instant I was on my feet with the cocked rifle to my shoulder—meaning to shoot before his charge, and then make good time up the tree. But there was no need. As I sprang to my feet he sprang for the hazel bushes, and went tearing through them with the speed of a deer, keeping up a succession of snorts and grunts that could be heard long after he had passed out of sight. I am not subject to buck fever, and was disgusted to find myself so badly "rattled" that I could scarcely handle the rifle. At first I was provoked at myself for not getting a good ready and shooting him in the head, as he came out of the bushes; but it was better to let him live. He was not carnivorous, or a beast of prey, and ugly as he was, certainly looked better alive than he would as a porcine corpse. No doubt he relished his acorns as well as though he had been less ugly, and he was a savage power in the forest. Bears love pork; and the fact that the hog was picking up a comfortable living in that wilderness, is presumptive evidence that he was a match for the largest bear, or he would have been eaten long before.

Another little incident, in which Bruin played a leading part, rises vividly to memory. It was hardly an adventure; only the meeting of man and bear, and they parted on good terms, with no hardness on either side.

The meeting occurred, as usually was the case with large game, on dry, oak lands, where the undergrowth was hazel, sassafras, and wild grapevine. As before, I had paused for a rest, when I began to catch glimpses of a very black animal working its way among the hazel bushes, under the scattering oaks, and toward me. With no definite intention of shooting, but just to see how easy it might be to kill him, I got a good ready, and waited. Slowly and lazily he nuzzled his way among the trees, sitting up occasionally to crunch acorns, until he was within twenty-five yards of me, with the bright bead neatly showing at the butt of his ear, and he sitting on his haunches, calmly chewing his acorns, oblivious of danger. He was the shortest-legged, blackest, and glossiest bear I had ever seen; and such a fair shot. But I could not use either skin or meat, and he was a splendid picture just as he sat. Shot down and left to taint the blessed air, he would not look as wholesome, let alone that it would be unwarrantable murder. And so, when he came nosing under the very tree where I was sitting, I suddenly jumped up, threw my hat at him, and gave a Comanche yell. He tumbled over in a limp heap, grunting and whining for very terror, gathered himself up, got up headway, and disappeared with wonderful speed—considering the length of his legs.

On another occasion—and this was in heavy timber—I was resting on a log, partially concealed by spice bushes, when I noticed a large flock of turkeys coming in my direction. As they rapidly advanced with their quick, gliding walk, the flock grew to a drove, the drove became a swarm—an army. To right and on the left, as far as I could see in front, a legion of turkeys were marching, steadily marching to the eastward. Among them were some of the grandest gobblers I had ever seen, and one magnificent fellow came straight toward me. Never before or since have I seen such a splendid wild bird. His thick, glossy black beard nearly reached the ground, his bronze uniform was of the richest, and he was decidedly the largest I have ever seen. When within fifty feet of the spot where I was nearly hidden, his wary eye caught something suspicious; and he raised his superb head for an instant in an attitude of motionless attention. Then, with lowered head and drooping tail, he turned right about, gave the note of alarm, put the trunk of a large tree quickly between himself and the enemy, and went away like the wind. With the speed of thought the warning note was sounded along the whole line, and in a moment the woods seemed alive with turkeys, running for dear life. In less time than it takes to tell it, that gallinaceous army had passed out of sight, forever. And the like of it will never again be possible on this continent.

And again, on the morning of the sixth day out, I blundered on to such an aggregation of deer as a man sees but once in a lifetime. I had camped over night on low land, among heavy timber, but soon after striking camp, came to a place where the timber was scattering, and the land had a gentle rise to the westward. Scarcely had I left the low land behind, when a few deer got out of their beds and commenced lazily bounding away. They were soon joined by others; on the right flank, on the left, and ahead, they continued to rise and canter off leisurely, stopping at a distance of one or two hundred yards to look back. It struck me finally that I had started something rather unusual, and I began counting the deer in sight. It was useless to attempt it; their white flags were flying in front and on both flanks, as far as one could see, and new ones seemed constantly joining the procession. Among them were several very large bucks with superb antlers, and these seemed very little afraid of the small, quiet biped in leaf-colored rig. They often paused to gaze back with bold, fearless front, as though inclined to call a halt and face the music; but when within a hundred yards, would turn and canter leisurely away. As the herd neared the summit of the low-lying ridge, I tried to make a reasonable guess at their numbers, by counting a part and estimating the rest, but could come to no satisfactory conclusion. As they passed the summit and loped down the gentle decline toward heavy timber, they began to scatter, and soon not a flag was in sight. It was a magnificent cervine army with white banners, and I shall never look upon its like again. The largest drove of deer I have seen in twenty years consisted of seven only.

And with much of interest, much of tramping, and not a little vexatious delay, I came at length to a stream that I knew must be the south branch of the Muskegon. The main river could scarcely be more than ten miles to the westward, and might be easily reached in one day.

It was time. The meal and pork were nearly gone, sugar and tea were at low ebb, and I was tired of venison; tired anyhow; ready for human speech and human companionship.

It was in the afternoon of the ninth day that I crossed the South Muskegon and laid a course west by north. The travelling was not bad; and in less than an hour I ran on to the ruins of a camp that I knew to be the work of Indians. It had evidently been a permanent winter camp, and was almost certainly the Indian camp spoken of by Bill Hance. Pausing a short time to look over the ruins, with the lonely feeling always induced by a decayed, rotting camp, I struck due west and made several miles before sundown.

I camped on a little rill, near a huge dry stub that would peel, made the last of the meal into a johnny-cake, broiled the last slice of pork, and lay down with the notion that a ten days' tramp, where it took an average of fifteen miles to make six, ought to end on the morrow. At sunrise I was again on foot, and after three hours of steady tramping, saw a smoky

opening ahead. In five minutes I was standing on the left
bank of the Muskegon.

And the Joe Davis camp—was it up stream or down? I decided on the latter, and started slowly down stream, keeping
an eye out for signs. In less than an hour I struck a dim log
road which led to the river, and there was a "landing," with
the usual debris of skids, loose bark, chocks, and some pieces
of broken boards. It did not take long to construct an efficient
log raft from the dry skids, and as I drifted placidly down
the deep, wild river, munching the last bit of johnny-cake, I
inwardly swore that my next wilderness cruise should be by
water.

It was in late afternoon that I heard—blessed sound—the
eager clank, clank, clank of the old-fashioned sawmill. It grew
nearer and more distinct; presently I could distinguish the
rumble of machinery as the carriage gigged back; then the
raft rounded a gentle bend, and a mill, with its long, log
boarding-house, came full in sight.

As the raft swung into the landing the mill became silent;
a brown-bearded, red-shirted fellow came down to welcome
me, a pair of strong hands grasped both my own, and the
voice of Joe Davis said earnestly, "Why, George! I never was
so d—d glad to see a man in my life!"

The ten days' tramp was ended. It had been wearisome to a
degree, but interesting and instructive. I had seen more game
birds and animals in the time than I ever saw before or since
in a whole season; and, though I came out with clothes pretty
well worn and torn off my back and legs, I was a little disposed
to plume myself on the achievement. Even at this day I am a
little proud of the fact that, with so many temptations to
slaughter, I only fired three shots on the route. Nothing but
the exceptionally fine, dry weather rendered such a trip possible in a wilderness so cut up with swamps, lakes, marshes
and streams. A week of steady rain or a premature snow
storm—either likely enough at that season—would have been
most disastrous; while a forest fire like that of '56, and later
ones, would simply have proved fatal.

Reader, if ever you are tempted to make a similar thought-
less, reckless trip—don't do it.

Chapter IX—Canoeing

THE LIGHT CANOE AND DOUBLE BLADE—VARIOUS CANOES FOR VARIOUS CANOEISTS—REASONS FOR PREFERRING THE CLINKER-BUILT CEDAR

 HE canoe is coming to the front, and canoeing is gaining rapidly in popular favor, in spite of the disparaging remark that "a canoe is a poor man's yacht." The canoe editor of *Forest and Stream* pertinently says, "we may as properly call a bicycle "the poor man's express train." But, suppose it is the poor man's yacht? Are we to be debarred from aquatic sports because we are not rich? And are we such weak flunkies as to be ashamed of poverty? Or to attempt shams and subterfuges to hide it? For myself, I freely accept the imputation. In common with nine-tenths of my fellow citizens I am poor—and the canoe is my yacht, as it would be were I a millionaire. We are a nation of many millions, and comparatively few of us are rich enough to support a yacht, let alone the fact that not one man in fifty lives near enough to yachting waters to make such an acquisition desirable—or feasible, even. It is different with the canoe. A man like myself may live in the backwoods, a hundred miles from a decent sized inland lake, and much further from the sea coast, and yet be an enthusiastic canoeist. For instance.

Last July I made my preparations for a canoe cruise, and spun out with as little delay as possible. I had pitched on the Adirondacks as cruising ground, and had more than 250 miles of railroads and buckboards to take, before launching the canoe on Moose River. She was carried thirteen miles over the Brown's Tract road on the head of her skipper, cruised from the western side of the Wilderness to the Lower St. Regis on the east side, cruised back again by a somewhat different route, was taken home to Pennsylvania on the cars, 250 miles, sent back to her builder, St. Lawrence County, N.Y., over 300 miles, thence by rail to New York City, where, the last I heard of her, she was on exhibition at the *Forest and Stream* office. She took her chances in the baggage car, with no special care, and is today, so far as I know, staunch and tight, with not a check in her frail siding.

Such cruising can only be made in a very light canoe, and with a very light outfit. It was sometimes necessary to make several carries in one day, aggregating as much as ten miles, besides from fifteen to twenty miles under paddle. No heavy, decked, paddling or sailing canoe would have been available for such a trip with a man of ordinary muscle.

The difference between a lone, independent cruise through an almost unbroken wilderness, and cruising along civilized routes, where the canoeist can interview farm houses and village groceries for supplies, getting gratuitous stonings from the small boy, and much reviling from ye ancient mariner of the towpath—I say, the difference is just immense. Whence it comes that I always prefer a very light, open canoe; one that I can carry almost as easily as my hat, and yet that will float me easily, buoyantly, and safely. And such a canoe was my last cruiser. She only weighed ten and one-half pounds when first launched, and after an all-summer rattling by land and water had only gained half a pound. I do not therefore advise any one to buy a ten and a half pound canoe; although she would prove competent for a skillful light-weight. She was built to order, as a test of lightness and was the third experiment in that line.

I have nothing to say against the really fine canoes that are in highest favor today. Were I fond of sailing, and satisfied to cruise on routes where clearings are more plentiful than carries, I dare say I should run a Shadow, or Stella Maris, at a cost of considerably more than $100—though I should hardly call it a "poor man's yacht."

Much is being said and written at the present day as to the

"perfect canoe." One writer decides in favor of a Pearl 15x31½ inches. In the same column another says, "the perfect canoe does not exist." I should rather say there are several types of the modern canoe, each nearly perfect in its way and for the use to which it is best adapted. The perfect paddling canoe is by no means perfect under canvas, and vice versa. The best cruiser is not a perfect racer, while neither of them is at all perfect as a paddling cruiser where much carrying is to be done. And the most perfect canoe for fishing and gunning around shallow, marshy waters, would be a very imperfect canoe for a rough and ready cruise of one hundred miles through a strange wilderness, where a day's cruise will sometimes include a dozen miles of carrying.

Believing, as I do, that the light, single canoe with double-bladed paddle is bound to soon become a leading—if not the leading—feature in summer recreation, and having been a light canoeist for nearly fifty years, during the last twenty of which I experimented much with the view of reducing weight, perhaps I can give some hints that may help a younger man in the selection of a canoe which shall be safe, pleasant to ride, and not burdensome to carry.

Let me promise that, up to four years ago, I was never able to get a canoe that entirely satisfied me as to weight and model. I bought the smallest birches I could find; procured a tiny Chippewa dugout from North Michigan, and once owned a kayak. They were all too heavy, and they were cranky to a degree.

About twenty years ago I commenced making my own canoes. The construction was of the simplest; a 22-inch pine board for the bottom, planed to ¾ of an inch thickness; two wide ½-inch boards for the sides, and two light oak stems; five pieces of wood in all. I found that the bend of the siding gave too much shear; for instance, if the siding was 12 inches wide, she would have a rise of 12 inches at stems and less than 5 inches at center. But the flat bottom made her very stiff, and for river work she was better than anything I had yet tried. She was too heavy, however, always weighing from 45 to 50 pounds, and awkward to carry.

My last canoe of this style went down the Susquehanna with

an ice jam in the spring of '79, and in the meantime canoeing
began to loom up. The best paper in the country which makes
out-door sport a specialty, devoted liberal space to canoeing,
and skilled boatbuilders were advertising canoes of various
models and widely different material. I commenced interview-
ing the builders by letter, and studying catalogues carefully.
There was a wide margin of choice. You could have lapstreak,
smooth skin, paper, veneer, or canvas. What I wanted was
light weight, and good model. I liked the Peterboro canoes;
they were decidedly canoey. Also, the veneered Racines; but
neither of them talked of a 20-pound canoe. The "Osgood
folding canvas" did. But I had some knowledge of canvas boats.
I knew they could make her down to 20 pounds. How much
would she weigh after being in the water a week, and how
would she behave when swamped in the middle of a lake, were
questions to be asked, for I always get swamped. One builder
of cedar canoes thought he could make me the boat I wanted,
inside of 20 pounds, clinker-built, and at my own risk, as he
hardly believed in so light a boat. I sent him the order, and
he turned out what is pretty well known in Brown's Tract as
the "Nessmuk canoe." She weighed just 17 pounds 13¾ ounces,
and was thought to be the lightest working canoe in existence.
Her builder gave me some advice about stiffening her with
braces, etc., if I found her too frail, "and he never expected
another like her."

"He builded better than he knew." She needed no bracing;
and she was, and is, a staunch, seaworthy little model. I fell
in love with her from the start. I had at last found the canoe
that I could ride in rough water, sleep in afloat, and carry
with ease for miles. I paddled her early and late, mainly on
the Fulton Chain; but I also cruised her on Raquette Lake,
Eagle, Utowana, Blue Mountain, and Forked Lakes. I paddled
her until there were black and blue streaks along the muscles
from wrist to elbow. Thank Heaven, I had found something
that made me a boy again. Her log shows a cruise for 1880 of
over 550 miles.

As regards her capacity (she is now on Third Lake, Brown's
Tract), James P. Fifield, a muscular young Forge House guide
of 6 feet 2 inches and 185 pounds weight, took her through the

Fulton Chain to Raquette Lake last summer; and, happening on his camp, Seventh Lake, last July, I asked him how she performed under his weight. He said, "I never made the trip to Raquette so lightly and easily in my life." And as to the opinion of her builder, he wrote me, under date of Nov. 18, '83: "I thought when I built the Nessmuk, no one else would ever want one. But I now build about a dozen of them a year. Great big men, ladies, and two, aye, three schoolboys ride in them. It is wonderful how few pounds of cedar, rightly modeled and properly put together, it takes to float a man." Just so, Mr. Builder. That's what I said when I ordered her. But few seemed to see it then.

The Nessmuk was by no means the ultimatum of lightness, and I ordered another six inches longer, two inches wider, and to weigh about 15 pounds. When she came to hand she was a beauty, finished in oil and shellac. But she weighed 16 pounds, and would not only carry me and my duffle, but I could easily carry a passenger of my weight. I cruised her in the summer of '81 over the Fulton Chain, Raquette Lake, Forked Lake, down the Raquette River, and on Long Lake. But her log only showed a record of 206 miles. The cruise that had been mapped for 600 miles was cut short by sickness, and I went into quarantine at the hostelry of Mitchell Sabattis. Slowly and feebly I crept back to the Fulton Chain, hung up at the Forge House, and the cruise of the Susan Nipper was ended. Later in the season, I sent for her, and she was forwarded by express, coming out over the fearful Brown's Tract road to Boonville (25½ miles) by buckboard. From Boonville home, she took her chances in the baggage car without protection, and reached her destination without a check or scratch. She hangs in her slings under the porch, a thing of beauty—and, like many beauties, a trifle frail—but staunch as the day I took her. Her proper lading is about 200 pounds. She can float 300 pounds.

Of my last and lightest venture, the Sairy Gamp, little more need be said. I will only add that a Mr. Dutton, of Philadelphia, got into her at the Forge House, and paddled her like an old canoeist, though it was his first experience with the double blade. He gave his age as sixty-four years, and weight, 140 pounds. Billy Cornell, a bright young guide, cruised her on Raquette

Lake quite as well as her owner could do it, and I thought she trimmed better with him. He paddled at 141½ pounds, which is just about her right lading. And she was only an experiment, anyhow. I wanted to find out how light a canoe it took to drown her skipper, and I do not yet know. I never shall. But, most of all, I desired to settle the question—approximately at least, of weight, as regards canoe and canoeist.

Many years ago, I became convinced that we were all, as canoeists, carrying and paddling just twice as much wood as was at all needful, and something more than a year since, I advanced the opinion in *Forest and Stream,* that ten pounds of well made cedar ought to carry one hundred pounds of man. The past season has more than proved it; but, as I may be a little exceptional, I leave myself out of the question, and have ordered my next canoe on lines and dimensions that, in my judgment, will be found nearly perfect for the average canoeist of 150 to 160 pounds. She will be much stronger than either of my other canoes, because few men would like a canoe so frail and limber that she can be sprung inward by hand pressure on the gunwales, as easily as a hat-box. And many men are clumsy or careless with a boat, while others are lubberly by nature. Her dimensions are: Length, 10½ feet; beam, 26 inches; rise at center, 9 inches; at seams, 15 inches; oval red elm ribs, 1 inch apart; an inch home tumble; stems, plumb and sharp; oak keel and keelson; clinker-built, of white cedar.

Such a canoe will weigh about 22 pounds, and will do just as well for the man of 140 or 170 pounds, while even a light weight of 110 pounds ought to take her over a portage with a light, elastic carrying frame, without distress. She will trim best, however, at about 160 pounds. For a welter, say of some 200 pounds, add 6 inches to her length, 2 inches to her beam, and 1 inch rise at center. The light weight canoeist will find that either of these two canoes will prove satisfactory, that is 10 feet in length, weight 16 pounds, or 10½ feet length, weight 18 pounds. Either is capable of 160 pounds, and they are very steady and buoyant, as I happen to know. I dare say any first class manufacturers will build canoes of these dimensions.

Provide your canoe with a flooring of oilcloth 3½ feet long by 15 inches wide; punch holes in it and tie it neatly to the ribbing, just where it will best protect the bottom from wear and danger. Use only a cushion for a seat, and do not buy a fancy one with permanent stuffing, but get sixpence worth of good, unbleached cotton cloth, and have it sewed into bag shape. Stuff the bag with fine browse, dry grass or leaves, settle it well together, and fasten the open end by turning it flatly back and using two or three pins. You can empty it if you like when going over a carry, and it makes a good pillow at night.

Select a canoe that fits you, just as you would a coat or hat. A 16-pound canoe may fit me exactly, but would be a bad misfit for a man of 180 pounds. And don't neglect the auxiliary paddle, or "pudding stick," as my friends call it. The notion may be new to most canoeists, but will be found exceedingly handy and useful. It is simply a little one-handed paddle weighing 5 to 7 ounces, 20 to 22 inches long, with a blade 3½ inches wide. Work it out of half-inch cherry or maple, and fine the blade down thin. Tie it to a rib with a slip-knot, having the handle in easy reach, and when you come to a narrow, tortuous channel, where shrubs and weeds crowd you on both sides, take the double-blade inboard, use the pudding stick, and you can go almost anywhere that a muskrat can.

In fishing for trout or floating deer, remember you are dealing with the wary, and that the broad blades are very showy in motion. Therefore, on approaching a spring-hole, lay the double-blade on the lily-pads where you can pick it up when wanted, and handle your canoe with the auxiliary. On hooking a large fish, handle the rod with one hand and with the other lay the canoe out into deep water, away from all entangling alliances. You may be surprised to find how easily, with a little practice, you can make a two-pound trout or bass tow the canoe the way you want it to go.

In floating for deer, use the double-blade only in making the passage to the ground; then take it apart and lay it inboard, using only the little paddle to float with, tying it to a rib with a yard and a half of linen line. On approaching a deer near enough to shoot, let go the paddle, leaving it to drift alongside while you attend to venison.

> Beneath a hemlock grim and dark,
> Where shrub and vine are intertwining,

Our shanty stands, well roofed with bark,
    On which the cheerful blaze is shining.
The smoke ascends in spiral wreath,
    With upward curve the sparks are trending;
The coffee kettle sings beneath
    Where sparks and smoke with leaves are blending.

And on the stream a light canoe
    Floats like a freshly fallen feather,
A fairy thing, that will not do
    For broader seas and stormy weather.
Her sides no thicker than the shell
    Of Ole Bull's Cremona fiddle,
The man who rides her will do well
    To part his scalp-lock in the middle.

                —"Forest Runes"—Nessmuk.

Chapter X

ODDS AND ENDS—WHERE TO GO FOR AN OUTING—
WHY A CLINKER?—BOUGHS AND BROWSE

T HE oft-recurring question as to where to go for the outing, can hardly be answered at all satisfactorily. In a general way, any place may, and ought to be, satisfactory, where there are fresh green woods, pleasant scenery, and fish and game plenty enough to supply the camp abundantly, with boating facilities and pure water.

"It's more in the man than it is in the land," and there are thousands of such places on the waters of the Susquehanna, the Delaware, the rivers and lakes of Maine, Michigan, Wisconsin, and Canada.

Among the lakes of Central New York one may easily select a camping ground, healthy, pleasant, easily reached, and with the advantage of cheapness. A little too much civilization, perhaps; but the farmers are friendly, and kindly disposed to all summer outers who behave like gentlemen.

For fine forest scenery and unequaled canoeing facilities, it must be admitted that the Adirondack region stands at the head. There is also fine fishing and good hunting, for those who know the right places to go for deer and trout. But it is a tedious, expensive job getting into the heart of the Wilderness, and it is the most costly woodland resort I know of when you are there. You can keep expenses down (and also have a much better sport) by avoiding the hotels and going into camp at once, and staying there. The best way is for two men to hire a guide, live in camp altogether, and divide the expense.

All along the Allegheny range, from Maine to Michigan, and

from Pennsylvania to the Provinces, numberless resorts exist as pleasant, as healthy, as prolific of sport, as the famed Adirondacks, and at half the cost. But, for an all-summer canoe cruise, with more than 600 accessible lakes and ponds, the Northern Wilderness stands alone. And, as a wealthy cockney once remarked to me in Brown's Tract, "It's no place for a poor man."

And now I will give my reasons for preferring the clinker-built cedar boat, or canoe, to any other. First, as to material. Cedar is stronger, more elastic, more enduring, and shrinks less than pine or any other light wood used as boat siding. As one of the best builders in the country says, "It has been thoroughly demonstrated that a cedar canoe will stand more hard knocks than an oak one; for where it only receives bruises, the oak streaks will split." And he might add, the pine will break. But I suppose it is settled beyond dispute that white cedar stands at the head for boat streaks. I prefer it, then, because it is the best. And I prefer the clinker, because it is the strongest, simplest, most enduring, and most easily repaired in case of accident. To prove the strength theory, take a cedar (or pine) strip eight feet long and six inches wide. Bend it to a certain point by an equal strain on each end, and carefully note the result. Next strip it lengthwise with the rip saw, lap the two halves an inch, and nail the lap as in boat building. Test it again, and you will find it has gained in strength about twenty per cent. That is the clinker of it.

Now work the laps down until the strip is of uniform thickness its entire length, and test it once more; you will find it much weaker than on first trial. That is the smooth skin, sometimes called lapstreak. They, the clinker canoes, are easily tightened when they spring a leak through being rattled over stones in rapids. It is only to hunt a smooth pebble for a clinch head, and settle the nails that have started with the hatchet, putting in a few new ones if needed. And they are put together, at least by the best builders, without any cement or white lead, naked wood to wood, and depending only on close work for waterproofing. And each pair of strips is cut to fit and lie in its proper place without strain, no two pairs being alike, but each pair, from garboards to upper streak, having easy, natural form for its destined position.

The veneered canoes are very fine, for deep water; but a few cuts on sharp stones will be found ruinous; and if exposed much to weather they are liable to warp. The builders understand this, and plainly say that they prefer not to build fine boats for those who will neglect the proper care of them.

The paper boat, also, will not stand much cutting on sharp stones, and it is not buoyant when swamped, unless fitted with water-tight compartments, which I abhor.

The canvas is rather a logy, limp sort of craft, to my thinking, and liable to drown her crew if swamped.

But each and all have their admirers, and purchasers as well, while each is good in its way, and I only mention a few reasons for my preference of the cedar.

When running an ugly rapid or crossing a stormy lake, I like to feel that I have enough light, seasoned wood under me to keep my mouth and nose above water all day, besides saving the rifle and knapsack, which, when running into danger, I always tie to the ribbing with strong linen line, as I do the paddle also, giving it about line enough to just allow free play.

I am not—to use a little modern slang—going to "give myself away" on canoeing, or talk of startling adventure. But, for the possible advantage of some future canoeist, I will briefly relate what happened to me on a certain windy morning one summer. It was on one of the larger lakes—no matter which—between Paul Smith's and the Fulton Chain. I had camped over night in a spot that did not suit me in the least, but it seemed the best I could do then and there. The night was rough, and the early morning threatening. However, I managed a cup of coffee, "tied in," and made a slippery carry of two miles a little after sunrise. Arrived on the shore of the lake, things did not look promising. The whirling, twirling clouds were black and dangerous looking, the crisp, dark waves were crested with spume, and I had a notion of just making a comfortable camp and waiting for better weather. But the commissary department was reduced to six Boston crackers, with a single slice of pork, and it was twelve miles of wilderness to the nearest point of supplies, four miles of it carries, included. Such weather might last a week, and I decided to go. For half an hour I sat on the beach, taking weather notes. The wind was northeast; my course was due west, giving me four points free. Taking five feet of strong line, I tied one end under a rib next the keelson, and the other around the paddle. Stripping to shirt and drawers, I stowed everything in the knapsack, and tied that safely in the fore peak. Then I swung out. Before I was a half mile out, I fervently wished myself back. But it was too late. How that little, corky, light canoe did bound and snap, with a constant tendency to come up in the wind'e eye, that kept me on the qui vive every instant. She shipped no mater; she was too buoyant for that. But she was all the time in danger of pitching her crew overboard. It soon came to a crisis. About the middle of the lake, on the north side, there is a sharp, low gulch that runs away back through the hills, looking like a level cut through a railroad embankment. And down this gulch came a fierce thunder gust that was like a small cyclone. It knocked down trees, swept over the lake, and—caught the little canoe on the crest of a wave, right under the garboard streak. I went overboard like a shot; but I kept my grip on the paddle. That grip was worth a thousand dollars to the "Travelers' Accidental"; and another thousand to the "Equitable Company," because the paddle, with its line, enabled me to keep the canoe in hand, and prevent her from going away to leeward like a dry leaf. When I once got my nose above water, and my hand on her after stem, I knew I had the whole business under control. Pressing the stem down, I took a look inboard. The little jilt! She had not shipped a quart of water. And there was the knapsack, the rod, the little auxiliary paddle, all just as I had tied them in; only the crew and the double-blade had gone overboard. As I am elderly and out of practice in the swimming line, and it was nearly half a mile to a lee shore, and, as I was out of breath and water-logged, it is quite possible that a little forethought and four cents' worth of fishline saved—the insurance companies two thousand dollars.

How I slowly kicked that canoe ashore; how the sun came out bright and hot; how, instead of making the remaining eleven miles, I raised a conflagration and a comfortable camp, dried out, and had a pleasant night of it; all this is neither here nor there. The point I wish to make is, keep your duffle safe to float, and your paddle and canoe sufficiently in hand to always hold your breathing works above water level. So shall your children look confidently for your safe return, while the "Accidentals" arise and call you a good investment.

There is only one objection to the clinker-built canoe that occurs to me as at all plausible. This is, that the ridge-like projections of her clinker laps offer resistance to the water, and retard her speed. Theoretically, this is correct. Practically, it is not proven. Her streaks are so nearly on her water line that the resistance, if any, must be infinitesimal. It is possible, however, that this element might lessen her speed one or two minutes in a mile race. I am not racing, but taking leisurely recreation. I can wait two or three minutes as well as not. Three or four knots an hour will take me through to the last carry quite as soon as I care to make the landing.

A few words of explanation and advice may not be out of place. I have used the words "boughs" and "browse" quite frequently. I am sorry they are not more in use. The first settlers in the unbroken forest knew how to diagnose a tree. They came to the "Holland Purchase" from the Eastern States, with their families, in a covered wagon, drawn by a yoke of oxen, and the favorite cow patiently leading behind. They could not start until the ground was settled, some time in May, and nothing could be done in late summer, save to erect a log cabin, and clear a few acres for the next season. To this end the oxen were indispensable, and a cow was of first necessity, where there were children. And cows and oxen must have hay. But there was not a ton of hay in the country. A few hundred pounds of coarse wild grass was gleaned from the margins of streams and small marshes; but the main reliance was "browse." Through the warm months the cattle could take care of themselves; but, when winter settled down in earnest, a large part of the settler's work consisted in providing browse for his cattle. First and best was the basswood (linden); then came maple, beech, birch and hemlock. Some of the trees would be nearly three feet in diameter, and, when felled, much of the browse would be twenty feet above the reach of cattle, on the ends of huge limbs. Then the boughs were lopped off, and the cattle could get at the browse. The settlers divided the tree into log, limbs, boughs, and browse. Anything small enough for a cow

or deer to masticate was browse. And that is just what you
want for a camp in the forest. Not twigs, that may come from
a thorn, or boughs, that may be as thick as your wrist, but
browse, which may be used for a mattress, the healthiest in the
world.

And now for a little useless advice. In going into the woods,
don't take a medicine chest or a set of surgical instruments
with you. A bit of sticking salve, a wooden vial of anti-pain
tablets and another of rhubarb regulars, your fly medicine, and
a pair of tweezers, will be enough. Of course you have needles
and thread.

If you go before the open season for shooting, take no gun.
It will simply be a useless incumbrance and a nuisance.

If you go to hunt, take a solemn oath never to point the
shooting end of your gun toward yourself or any other human
being.

In still-hunting, swear yourself black in the face never to
shoot at a dim, moving object in the woods for a deer, unless
you have seen that it is a deer. In these days there are quite
as many hunters as deer in the woods; and it is a heavy, wearisome job to pack a dead or wounded man ten or twelve miles
out to a clearing, let alone that it spoils all the pleasure of the
hunt, and is apt to raise hard feelings among his relations.

In a word, act coolly and rationally. So shall your outing be
a delight in conception and the fulfillment thereof; while the
memory of it shall come back to you in pleasant dreams, when
legs and shoulders are too stiff and old for knapsack and rifle.

That is me. That is why I sit here tonight—with the north
wind and sleet rattling the one window of my little den—
writing what I hope younger and stronger men will like to
take into the woods with them, and read. Not that I am so
very old. The youngsters are still not anxious to buck against
the muzzleloader in off-hand shooting. But, in common with a
thousand other old graybeards, I feel that the fire, the fervor,
the steel, that once carried me over the trail from dawn until
dark, is dulled and deadened within me.

> We had our day of youth and May;
>   We may have grown a trifle sober;
> But life may reach a wintry way,
>   And we are only in October.

Wherefore, let us be thankful that there are still thousands of cool, green nooks beside crystal springs, where the weary soul may hide for a time, away from debts, duns and deviltries, and a while commune with nature in her undress.

And with kindness to all true woodsmen; and with malice toward none, save the trout-hog, the netter, the cruster, and skin-butcher, let us

PREPARE TO TURN IN.

Index

A CATALOG OF SELECTED
DOVER BOOKS
IN ALL FIELDS OF INTEREST

A CATALOG OF SELECTED DOVER
BOOKS IN ALL FIELDS OF INTEREST

CONCERNING THE SPIRITUAL IN ART, Wassily Kandinsky. Pioneering work by father of abstract art. Thoughts on color theory, nature of art. Analysis of earlier masters. 12 illustrations. 80pp. of text. 5⅜ x 8½. 0-486-23411-8

CELTIC ART: The Methods of Construction, George Bain. Simple geometric techniques for making Celtic interlacements, spirals, Kells-type initials, animals, humans, etc. Over 500 illustrations. 160pp. 9 x 12. (Available in U.S. only.) 0-486-22923-8

AN ATLAS OF ANATOMY FOR ARTISTS, Fritz Schider. Most thorough reference work on art anatomy in the world. Hundreds of illustrations, including selections from works by Vesalius, Leonardo, Goya, Ingres, Michelangelo, others. 593 illustrations. 192pp. 7⅛ x 10¼. 0-486-20241-0

CELTIC HAND STROKE-BY-STROKE (Irish Half-Uncial from "The Book of Kells"): An Arthur Baker Calligraphy Manual, Arthur Baker. Complete guide to creating each letter of the alphabet in distinctive Celtic manner. Covers hand position, strokes, pens, inks, paper, more. Illustrated. 48pp. 8¼ x 11. 0-486-24336-2

EASY ORIGAMI, John Montroll. Charming collection of 32 projects (hat, cup, pelican, piano, swan, many more) specially designed for the novice origami hobbyist. Clearly illustrated easy-to-follow instructions insure that even beginning papercrafters will achieve successful results. 48pp. 8¼ x 11. 0-486-27298-2

BLOOMINGDALE'S ILLUSTRATED 1886 CATALOG: Fashions, Dry Goods and Housewares, Bloomingdale Brothers. Famed merchants' extremely rare catalog depicting about 1,700 products: clothing, housewares, firearms, dry goods, jewelry, more. Invaluable for dating, identifying vintage items. Also, copyright-free graphics for artists, designers. Co-published with Henry Ford Museum & Greenfield Village. 160pp. 8¼ x 11. 0-486-25780-0

THE ART OF WORLDLY WISDOM, Baltasar Gracian. "Think with the few and speak with the many," "Friends are a second existence," and "Be able to forget" are among this 1637 volume's 300 pithy maxims. A perfect source of mental and spiritual refreshment, it can be opened at random and appreciated either in brief or at length. 128pp. 5⅜ x 8½. 0-486-44034-6

JOHNSON'S DICTIONARY: A Modern Selection, Samuel Johnson (E. L. McAdam and George Milne, eds.). This modern version reduces the original 1755 edition's 2,300 pages of definitions and literary examples to a more manageable length, retaining the verbal pleasure and historical curiosity of the original. 480pp. 5³⁄₁₆ x 8¼. 0-486-44089-3

ADVENTURES OF HUCKLEBERRY FINN, Mark Twain, Illustrated by E. W. Kemble. A work of eternal richness and complexity, a source of ongoing critical debate, and a literary landmark, Twain's 1885 masterpiece about a barefoot boy's journey of self-discovery has enthralled readers around the world. This handsome clothbound reproduction of the first edition features all 174 of the original black-and-white illustrations. 368pp. 5⅜ x 8½. 0-486-44322-1

CATALOG OF DOVER BOOKS

THE CLARINET AND CLARINET PLAYING, David Pino. Lively, comprehensive work features suggestions about technique, musicianship, and musical interpretation, as well as guidelines for teaching, making your own reeds, and preparing for public performance. Includes an intriguing look at clarinet history. "A godsend," *The Clarinet,* Journal of the International Clarinet Society. Appendixes. 7 illus. 320pp. 5⅜ x 8½. 0-486-40270-3

HOLLYWOOD GLAMOR PORTRAITS, John Kobal (ed.). 145 photos from 1926-49. Harlow, Gable, Bogart, Bacall; 94 stars in all. Full background on photographers, technical aspects. 160pp. 8⅜ x 11¼. 0-486-23352-9

THE RAVEN AND OTHER FAVORITE POEMS, Edgar Allan Poe. Over 40 of the author's most memorable poems: "The Bells," "Ulalume," "Israfel," "To Helen," "The Conqueror Worm," "Eldorado," "Annabel Lee," many more. Alphabetic lists of titles and first lines. 64pp. 5⁵⁄₁₆ x 8¼. 0-486-26685-0

PERSONAL MEMOIRS OF U. S. GRANT, Ulysses Simpson Grant. Intelligent, deeply moving firsthand account of Civil War campaigns, considered by many the finest military memoirs ever written. Includes letters, historic photographs, maps and more. 528pp. 6⅛ x 9¼. 0-486-28587-1

ANCIENT EGYPTIAN MATERIALS AND INDUSTRIES, A. Lucas and J. Harris. Fascinating, comprehensive, thoroughly documented text describes this ancient civilization's vast resources and the processes that incorporated them in daily life, including the use of animal products, building materials, cosmetics, perfumes and incense, fibers, glazed ware, glass and its manufacture, materials used in the mummification process, and much more. 544pp. 6⅛ x 9¼. (Available in U.S. only.) 0-486-40446-3

RUSSIAN STORIES/RUSSKIE RASSKAZY: A Dual-Language Book, edited by Gleb Struve. Twelve tales by such masters as Chekhov, Tolstoy, Dostoevsky, Pushkin, others. Excellent word-for-word English translations on facing pages, plus teaching and study aids, Russian/English vocabulary, biographical/critical introductions, more. 416pp. 5⅜ x 8½. 0-486-26244-8

PHILADELPHIA THEN AND NOW: 60 Sites Photographed in the Past and Present, Kenneth Finkel and Susan Oyama. Rare photographs of City Hall, Logan Square, Independence Hall, Betsy Ross House, other landmarks juxtaposed with contemporary views. Captures changing face of historic city. Introduction. Captions. 128pp. 8¼ x 11. 0-486-25790-8

NORTH AMERICAN INDIAN LIFE: Customs and Traditions of 23 Tribes, Elsie Clews Parsons (ed.). 27 fictionalized essays by noted anthropologists examine religion, customs, government, additional facets of life among the Winnebago, Crow, Zuni, Eskimo, other tribes. 480pp. 6⅛ x 9¼. 0-486-27377-6

TECHNICAL MANUAL AND DICTIONARY OF CLASSICAL BALLET, Gail Grant. Defines, explains, comments on steps, movements, poses and concepts. 15-page pictorial section. Basic book for student, viewer. 127pp. 5⅜ x 8½. 0-486-21843-0

THE MALE AND FEMALE FIGURE IN MOTION: 60 Classic Photographic Sequences, Eadweard Muybridge. 60 true-action photographs of men and women walking, running, climbing, bending, turning, etc., reproduced from rare 19th-century masterpiece. vi + 121pp. 9 x 12. 0-486-24745-7

ANIMALS: 1,419 Copyright-Free Illustrations of Mammals, Birds, Fish, Insects, etc., Jim Harter (ed.). Clear wood engravings present, in extremely lifelike poses, over 1,000 species of animals. One of the most extensive pictorial sourcebooks of its kind. Captions. Index. 284pp. 9 x 12. 0-486-23766-4

1001 QUESTIONS ANSWERED ABOUT THE SEASHORE, N. J. Berrill and Jacquelyn Berrill. Queries answered about dolphins, sea snails, sponges, starfish, fishes, shore birds, many others. Covers appearance, breeding, growth, feeding, much more. 305pp. 5¼ x 8¼. 0-486-23366-9

ATTRACTING BIRDS TO YOUR YARD, William J. Weber. Easy-to-follow guide offers advice on how to attract the greatest diversity of birds: birdhouses, feeders, water and waterers, much more. 96pp. 5³⁄₁₆ x 8¼. 0-486-28927-3

MEDICINAL AND OTHER USES OF NORTH AMERICAN PLANTS: A Historical Survey with Special Reference to the Eastern Indian Tribes, Charlotte Erichsen-Brown. Chronological historical citations document 500 years of usage of plants, trees, shrubs native to eastern Canada, northeastern U.S. Also complete identifying information. 343 illustrations. 544pp. 6½ x 9¼. 0-486-25951-X

STORYBOOK MAZES, Dave Phillips. 23 stories and mazes on two-page spreads: Wizard of Oz, Treasure Island, Robin Hood, etc. Solutions. 64pp. 8¼ x 11. 0-486-23628-5

AMERICAN NEGRO SONGS: 230 Folk Songs and Spirituals, Religious and Secular, John W. Work. This authoritative study traces the African influences of songs sung and played by black Americans at work, in church, and as entertainment. The author discusses the lyric significance of such songs as "Swing Low, Sweet Chariot," "John Henry," and others and offers the words and music for 230 songs. Bibliography. Index of Song Titles. 272pp. 6½ x 9¼. 0-486-40271-1

MOVIE-STAR PORTRAITS OF THE FORTIES, John Kobal (ed.). 163 glamor, studio photos of 106 stars of the 1940s: Rita Hayworth, Ava Gardner, Marlon Brando, Clark Gable, many more. 176pp. 8⅜ x 11¼. 0-486-23546-7

YEKL and THE IMPORTED BRIDEGROOM AND OTHER STORIES OF YIDDISH NEW YORK, Abraham Cahan. Film Hester Street based on *Yekl* (1896). Novel, other stories among first about Jewish immigrants on N.Y.'s East Side. 240pp. 5⅜ x 8½. 0-486-22427-9

SELECTED POEMS, Walt Whitman. Generous sampling from *Leaves of Grass*. Twenty-four poems include "I Hear America Singing," "Song of the Open Road," "I Sing the Body Electric," "When Lilacs Last in the Dooryard Bloom'd," "O Captain! My Captain!"–all reprinted from an authoritative edition. Lists of titles and first lines. 128pp. 5³⁄₁₆ x 8¼. 0-486-26878-0

SONGS OF EXPERIENCE: Facsimile Reproduction with 26 Plates in Full Color, William Blake. 26 full-color plates from a rare 1826 edition. Includes "The Tyger," "London," "Holy Thursday," and other poems. Printed text of poems. 48pp. 5¼ x 7. 0-486-24636-1

THE BEST TALES OF HOFFMANN, E. T. A. Hoffmann. 10 of Hoffmann's most important stories: "Nutcracker and the King of Mice," "The Golden Flowerpot," etc. 458pp. 5⅜ x 8½. 0-486-21793-0

THE BOOK OF TEA, Kakuzo Okakura. Minor classic of the Orient: entertaining, charming explanation, interpretation of traditional Japanese culture in terms of tea ceremony. 94pp. 5⅜ x 8½. 0-486-20070-1

FRENCH STORIES/CONTES FRANÇAIS: A Dual-Language Book, Wallace Fowlie. Ten stories by French masters, Voltaire to Camus: "Micromegas" by Voltaire; "The Atheist's Mass" by Balzac; "Minuet" by de Maupassant; "The Guest" by Camus, six more. Excellent English translations on facing pages. Also French-English vocabulary list, exercises, more. 352pp. 5⅜ x 8½. 0-486-26443-2

CHICAGO AT THE TURN OF THE CENTURY IN PHOTOGRAPHS: 122 Historic Views from the Collections of the Chicago Historical Society, Larry A. Viskochil. Rare large-format prints offer detailed views of City Hall, State Street, the Loop, Hull House, Union Station, many other landmarks, circa 1904-1913. Introduction. Captions. Maps. 144pp. 9⅜ x 12¼. 0-486-24656-6

OLD BROOKLYN IN EARLY PHOTOGRAPHS, 1865-1929, William Lee Younger. Luna Park, Gravesend race track, construction of Grand Army Plaza, moving of Hotel Brighton, etc. 157 previously unpublished photographs. 165pp. 8⅞ x 11¾. 0-486-23587-4

THE MYTHS OF THE NORTH AMERICAN INDIANS, Lewis Spence. Rich anthology of the myths and legends of the Algonquins, Iroquois, Pawnees and Sioux, prefaced by an extensive historical and ethnological commentary. 36 illustrations. 480pp. 5⅜ x 8½. 0-486-25967-6

AN ENCYCLOPEDIA OF BATTLES: Accounts of Over 1,560 Battles from 1479 B.C. to the Present, David Eggenberger. Essential details of every major battle in recorded history from the first battle of Megiddo in 1479 B.C. to Grenada in 1984. List of Battle Maps. New Appendix covering the years 1967-1984. Index. 99 illustrations. 544pp. 6½ x 9¼. 0-486-24913-1

SAILING ALONE AROUND THE WORLD, Captain Joshua Slocum. First man to sail around the world, alone, in small boat. One of great feats of seamanship told in delightful manner. 67 illustrations. 294pp. 5⅜ x 8½. 0-486-20326-3

ANARCHISM AND OTHER ESSAYS, Emma Goldman. Powerful, penetrating, prophetic essays on direct action, role of minorities, prison reform, puritan hypocrisy, violence, etc. 271pp. 5⅜ x 8½. 0-486-22484-8

MYTHS OF THE HINDUS AND BUDDHISTS, Ananda K. Coomaraswamy and Sister Nivedita. Great stories of the epics; deeds of Krishna, Shiva, taken from puranas, Vedas, folk tales; etc. 32 illustrations. 400pp. 5⅜ x 8½. 0-486-21759-0

MY BONDAGE AND MY FREEDOM, Frederick Douglass. Born a slave, Douglass became outspoken force in antislavery movement. The best of Douglass' autobiographies. Graphic description of slave life. 464pp. 5⅜ x 8½. 0-486-22457-0

FOLLOWING THE EQUATOR: A Journey Around the World, Mark Twain. Fascinating humorous account of 1897 voyage to Hawaii, Australia, India, New Zealand, etc. Ironic, bemused reports on peoples, customs, climate, flora and fauna, politics, much more. 197 illustrations. 720pp. 5⅜ x 8½. 0-486-26113-1

THE PEOPLE CALLED SHAKERS, Edward D. Andrews. Definitive study of Shakers: origins, beliefs, practices, dances, social organization, furniture and crafts, etc. 33 illustrations. 351pp. 5⅜ x 8½. 0-486-21081-2

THE MYTHS OF GREECE AND ROME, H. A. Guerber. A classic of mythology, generously illustrated, long prized for its simple, graphic, accurate retelling of the principal myths of Greece and Rome, and for its commentary on their origins and significance. With 64 illustrations by Michelangelo, Raphael, Titian, Rubens, Canova, Bernini and others. 480pp. 5⅜ x 8½. 0-486-27584-1

PSYCHOLOGY OF MUSIC, Carl E. Seashore. Classic work discusses music as a medium from psychological viewpoint. Clear treatment of physical acoustics, auditory apparatus, sound perception, development of musical skills, nature of musical feeling, host of other topics. 88 figures. 408pp. 5⅜ x 8½. 0-486-21851-1

LIFE IN ANCIENT EGYPT, Adolf Erman. Fullest, most thorough, detailed older account with much not in more recent books, domestic life, religion, magic, medicine, commerce, much more. Many illustrations reproduce tomb paintings, carvings, hieroglyphs, etc. 597pp. 5⅜ x 8½. 0-486-22632-8

SUNDIALS, Their Theory and Construction, Albert Waugh. Far and away the best, most thorough coverage of ideas, mathematics concerned, types, construction, adjusting anywhere. Simple, nontechnical treatment allows even children to build several of these dials. Over 100 illustrations. 230pp. 5⅜ x 8½. 0-486-22947-5

THEORETICAL HYDRODYNAMICS, L. M. Milne-Thomson. Classic exposition of the mathematical theory of fluid motion, applicable to both hydrodynamics and aerodynamics. Over 600 exercises. 768pp. 6⅛ x 9¼. 0-486-68970-0

OLD-TIME VIGNETTES IN FULL COLOR, Carol Belanger Grafton (ed.). Over 390 charming, often sentimental illustrations, selected from archives of Victorian graphics—pretty women posing, children playing, food, flowers, kittens and puppies, smiling cherubs, birds and butterflies, much more. All copyright-free. 48pp. 9¼ x 12¼. 0-486-27269-9

PERSPECTIVE FOR ARTISTS, Rex Vicat Cole. Depth, perspective of sky and sea, shadows, much more, not usually covered. 391 diagrams, 81 reproductions of drawings and paintings. 279pp. 5⅜ x 8½. 0-486-22487-2

DRAWING THE LIVING FIGURE, Joseph Sheppard. Innovative approach to artistic anatomy focuses on specifics of surface anatomy, rather than muscles and bones. Over 170 drawings of live models in front, back and side views, and in widely varying poses. Accompanying diagrams. 177 illustrations. Introduction. Index. 144pp. 8⅜ x11¼. 0-486-26723-7

GOTHIC AND OLD ENGLISH ALPHABETS: 100 Complete Fonts, Dan X. Solo. Add power, elegance to posters, signs, other graphics with 100 stunning copyright-free alphabets: Blackstone, Dolbey, Germania, 97 more—including many lower-case, numerals, punctuation marks. 104pp. 8⅛ x 11. 0-486-24695-7

THE BOOK OF WOOD CARVING, Charles Marshall Sayers. Finest book for beginners discusses fundamentals and offers 34 designs. "Absolutely first rate . . . well thought out and well executed."–E. J. Tangerman. 118pp. 7¾ x 10⅝. 0-486-23654-4

ILLUSTRATED CATALOG OF CIVIL WAR MILITARY GOODS: Union Army Weapons, Insignia, Uniform Accessories, and Other Equipment, Schuyler, Hartley, and Graham. Rare, profusely illustrated 1846 catalog includes Union Army uniform and dress regulations, arms and ammunition, coats, insignia, flags, swords, rifles, etc. 226 illustrations. 160pp. 9 x 12. 0-486-24939-5

WOMEN'S FASHIONS OF THE EARLY 1900s: An Unabridged Republication of "New York Fashions, 1909," National Cloak & Suit Co. Rare catalog of mail-order fashions documents women's and children's clothing styles shortly after the turn of the century. Captions offer full descriptions, prices. Invaluable resource for fashion, costume historians. Approximately 725 illustrations. 128pp. 8⅜ x 11¼. 0-486-27276-1

HOW TO DO BEADWORK, Mary White. Fundamental book on craft from simple projects to five-bead chains and woven works. 106 illustrations. 142pp. 5⅜ x 8.

0-486-20697-1

THE 1912 AND 1915 GUSTAV STICKLEY FURNITURE CATALOGS, Gustav Stickley. With over 200 detailed illustrations and descriptions, these two catalogs are essential reading and reference materials and identification guides for Stickley furniture. Captions cite materials, dimensions and prices. 112pp. 6½ x 9¼. 0-486-26676-1

EARLY AMERICAN LOCOMOTIVES, John H. White, Jr. Finest locomotive engravings from early 19th century: historical (1804–74), main-line (after 1870), special, foreign, etc. 147 plates. 142pp. 11⅜ x 8¼. 0-486-22772-3

LITTLE BOOK OF EARLY AMERICAN CRAFTS AND TRADES, Peter Stockham (ed.). 1807 children's book explains crafts and trades: baker, hatter, cooper, potter, and many others. 23 copperplate illustrations. 140pp. 4⁵/₈ x 6.

0-486-23336-7

VICTORIAN FASHIONS AND COSTUMES FROM HARPER'S BAZAR, 1867–1898, Stella Blum (ed.). Day costumes, evening wear, sports clothes, shoes, hats, other accessories in over 1,000 detailed engravings. 320pp. 9⅜ x 12¼.

0-486-22990-4

THE LONG ISLAND RAIL ROAD IN EARLY PHOTOGRAPHS, Ron Ziel. Over 220 rare photos, informative text document origin (1844) and development of rail service on Long Island. Vintage views of early trains, locomotives, stations, passengers, crews, much more. Captions. 8⅞ x 11¾. 0-486-26301-0

VOYAGE OF THE LIBERDADE, Joshua Slocum. Great 19th-century mariner's thrilling, first-hand account of the wreck of his ship off South America, the 35-foot boat he built from the wreckage, and its remarkable voyage home. 128pp. 5⅜ x 8½.

0-486-40022-0

TEN BOOKS ON ARCHITECTURE, Vitruvius. The most important book ever written on architecture. Early Roman aesthetics, technology, classical orders, site selection, all other aspects. Morgan translation. 331pp. 5⅜ x 8½. 0-486-20645-9

THE HUMAN FIGURE IN MOTION, Eadweard Muybridge. More than 4,500 stopped-action photos, in action series, showing undraped men, women, children jumping, lying down, throwing, sitting, wrestling, carrying, etc. 390pp. 7⅞ x 10⅝.

0-486-20204-6 Clothbd.

TREES OF THE EASTERN AND CENTRAL UNITED STATES AND CANADA, William M. Harlow. Best one-volume guide to 140 trees. Full descriptions, woodlore, range, etc. Over 600 illustrations. Handy size. 288pp. 4½ x 6⅜. 0-486-20395-6

GROWING AND USING HERBS AND SPICES, Milo Miloradovich. Versatile handbook provides all the information needed for cultivation and use of all the herbs and spices available in North America. 4 illustrations. Index. Glossary. 236pp. 5⅜ x 8½.

0-486-25058-X

BIG BOOK OF MAZES AND LABYRINTHS, Walter Shepherd. 50 mazes and labyrinths in all–classical, solid, ripple, and more–in one great volume. Perfect inexpensive puzzler for clever youngsters. Full solutions. 112pp. 8⅛ x 11. 0-486-22951-3

PIANO TUNING, J. Cree Fischer. Clearest, best book for beginner, amateur. Simple repairs, raising dropped notes, tuning by easy method of flattened fifths. No previous skills needed. 4 illustrations. 201pp. 5⅜ x 8½. 0-486-23267-0

HINTS TO SINGERS, Lillian Nordica. Selecting the right teacher, developing confidence, overcoming stage fright, and many other important skills receive thoughtful discussion in this indispensible guide, written by a world-famous diva of four decades' experience. 96pp. 5⅜ x 8½.   0-486-40094-8

THE COMPLETE NONSENSE OF EDWARD LEAR, Edward Lear. All nonsense limericks, zany alphabets, Owl and Pussycat, songs, nonsense botany, etc., illustrated by Lear. Total of 320pp. 5⅜ x 8½. (Available in U.S. only.)   0-486-20167-8

VICTORIAN PARLOUR POETRY: An Annotated Anthology, Michael R. Turner. 117 gems by Longfellow, Tennyson, Browning, many lesser-known poets. "The Village Blacksmith," "Curfew Must Not Ring Tonight," "Only a Baby Small," dozens more, often difficult to find elsewhere. Index of poets, titles, first lines. xxiii + 325pp. 5⅜ x 8¼.   0-486-27044-0

DUBLINERS, James Joyce. Fifteen stories offer vivid, tightly focused observations of the lives of Dublin's poorer classes. At least one, "The Dead," is considered a masterpiece. Reprinted complete and unabridged from standard edition. 160pp. 5³⁄₁₆ x 8¼.
                                                                     0-486-26870-5

GREAT WEIRD TALES: 14 Stories by Lovecraft, Blackwood, Machen and Others, S. T. Joshi (ed.). 14 spellbinding tales, including "The Sin Eater," by Fiona McLeod, "The Eye Above the Mantel," by Frank Belknap Long, as well as renowned works by R. H. Barlow, Lord Dunsany, Arthur Machen, W. C. Morrow and eight other masters of the genre. 256pp. 5⅜ x 8½. (Available in U.S. only.)   0-486-40436-6

THE BOOK OF THE SACRED MAGIC OF ABRAMELIN THE MAGE, translated by S. MacGregor Mathers. Medieval manuscript of ceremonial magic. Basic document in Aleister Crowley, Golden Dawn groups. 268pp. 5⅜ x 8½.
                                                                     0-486-23211-5

THE BATTLES THAT CHANGED HISTORY, Fletcher Pratt. Eminent historian profiles 16 crucial conflicts, ancient to modern, that changed the course of civilization. 352pp. 5⅜ x 8½.   0-486-41129-X

NEW RUSSIAN-ENGLISH AND ENGLISH-RUSSIAN DICTIONARY, M. A. O'Brien. This is a remarkably handy Russian dictionary, containing a surprising amount of information, including over 70,000 entries. 366pp. 4½ x 6⅛.
                                                                     0-486-20208-9

NEW YORK IN THE FORTIES, Andreas Feininger. 162 brilliant photographs by the well-known photographer, formerly with *Life* magazine. Commuters, shoppers, Times Square at night, much else from city at its peak. Captions by John von Hartz. 181pp. 9¼ x 10¾.   0-486-23585-8

INDIAN SIGN LANGUAGE, William Tomkins. Over 525 signs developed by Sioux and other tribes. Written instructions and diagrams. Also 290 pictographs. 111pp. 6⅛ x 9¼.   0-486-22029-X

ANATOMY: A Complete Guide for Artists, Joseph Sheppard. A master of figure drawing shows artists how to render human anatomy convincingly. Over 460 illustrations. 224pp. 8⅜ x 11¼.   0-486-27279-6

MEDIEVAL CALLIGRAPHY: Its History and Technique, Marc Drogin. Spirited history, comprehensive instruction manual covers 13 styles (ca. 4th century through 15th). Excellent photographs; directions for duplicating medieval techniques with modern tools. 224pp. 8⅜ x 11¼.   0-486-26142-5

DRIED FLOWERS: How to Prepare Them, Sarah Whitlock and Martha Rankin. Complete instructions on how to use silica gel, meal and borax, perlite aggregate, sand and borax, glycerine and water to create attractive permanent flower arrangements. 12 illustrations. 32pp. 5⅜ x 8½. 0-486-21802-3

EASY-TO-MAKE BIRD FEEDERS FOR WOODWORKERS, Scott D. Campbell. Detailed, simple-to-use guide for designing, constructing, caring for and using feeders. Text, illustrations for 12 classic and contemporary designs. 96pp. 5⅜ x 8½. 0-486-25847-5

THE COMPLETE BOOK OF BIRDHOUSE CONSTRUCTION FOR WOOD-WORKERS, Scott D. Campbell. Detailed instructions, illustrations, tables. Also data on bird habitat and instinct patterns. Bibliography. 3 tables. 63 illustrations in 15 figures. 48pp. 5¼ x 8½. 0-486-24407-5

SCOTTISH WONDER TALES FROM MYTH AND LEGEND, Donald A. Mackenzie. 16 lively tales tell of giants rumbling down mountainsides, of a magic wand that turns stone pillars into warriors, of gods and goddesses, evil hags, powerful forces and more. 240pp. 5⅜ x 8½. 0-486-29677-6

THE HISTORY OF UNDERCLOTHES, C. Willett Cunnington and Phyllis Cunnington. Fascinating, well-documented survey covering six centuries of English undergarments, enhanced with over 100 illustrations: 12th-century laced-up bodice, footed long drawers (1795), 19th-century bustles, 19th-century corsets for men, Victorian "bust improvers," much more. 272pp. 5⅜ x 8¼. 0-486-27124-2

ARTS AND CRAFTS FURNITURE: The Complete Brooks Catalog of 1912, Brooks Manufacturing Co. Photos and detailed descriptions of more than 150 now very collectible furniture designs from the Arts and Crafts movement depict davenports, settees, buffets, desks, tables, chairs, bedsteads, dressers and more, all built of solid, quarter-sawed oak. Invaluable for students and enthusiasts of antiques, Americana and the decorative arts. 80pp. 6½ x 9¼. 0-486-27471-3

WILBUR AND ORVILLE: A Biography of the Wright Brothers, Fred Howard. Definitive, crisply written study tells the full story of the brothers' lives and work. A vividly written biography, unparalleled in scope and color, that also captures the spirit of an extraordinary era. 560pp. 6⅛ x 9¼. 0-486-40297-5

THE ARTS OF THE SAILOR: Knotting, Splicing and Ropework, Hervey Garrett Smith. Indispensable shipboard reference covers tools, basic knots and useful hitches; handsewing and canvas work, more. Over 100 illustrations. Delightful reading for sea lovers. 256pp. 5⅜ x 8½. 0-486-26440-8

FRANK LLOYD WRIGHT'S FALLINGWATER: The House and Its History, Second, Revised Edition, Donald Hoffmann. A total revision—both in text and illustrations—of the standard document on Fallingwater, the boldest, most personal architectural statement of Wright's mature years, updated with valuable new material from the recently opened Frank Lloyd Wright Archives. "Fascinating"–*The New York Times.* 116 illustrations. 128pp. 9¼ x 10¾. 0-486-27430-6

PHOTOGRAPHIC SKETCHBOOK OF THE CIVIL WAR, Alexander Gardner. 100 photos taken on field during the Civil War. Famous shots of Manassas Harper's Ferry, Lincoln, Richmond, slave pens, etc. 244pp. 10⅝ x 8¼. 0-486-22731-6

FIVE ACRES AND INDEPENDENCE, Maurice G. Kains. Great back-to-the-land classic explains basics of self-sufficient farming. The one book to get. 95 illustrations. 397pp. 5⅜ x 8½. 0-486-20974-1

A MODERN HERBAL, Margaret Grieve. Much the fullest, most exact, most useful compilation of herbal material. Gigantic alphabetical encyclopedia, from aconite to zedoary, gives botanical information, medical properties, folklore, economic uses, much else. Indispensable to serious reader. 161 illustrations. 888pp. 6½ x 9¼. 2-vol. set. (Available in U.S. only.)   Vol. I: 0-486-22798-7   Vol. II: 0-486-22799-5

HIDDEN TREASURE MAZE BOOK, Dave Phillips. Solve 34 challenging mazes accompanied by heroic tales of adventure. Evil dragons, people-eating plants, blood-thirsty giants, many more dangerous adversaries lurk at every twist and turn. 34 mazes, stories, solutions. 48pp. 8¼ x 11.   0-486-24566-7

LETTERS OF W. A. MOZART, Wolfgang A. Mozart. Remarkable letters show bawdy wit, humor, imagination, musical insights, contemporary musical world; includes some letters from Leopold Mozart. 276pp. 5⅜ x 8½.   0-486-22859-2

BASIC PRINCIPLES OF CLASSICAL BALLET, Agrippina Vaganova. Great Russian theoretician, teacher explains methods for teaching classical ballet. 118 illustrations. 175pp. 5⅜ x 8½.   0-486-22036-2

THE JUMPING FROG, Mark Twain. Revenge edition. The original story of The Celebrated Jumping Frog of Calaveras County, a hapless French translation, and Twain's hilarious "retranslation" from the French. 12 illustrations. 66pp. 5⅜ x 8½.

0-486-22686-7

BEST REMEMBERED POEMS, Martin Gardner (ed.). The 126 poems in this superb collection of 19th- and 20th-century British and American verse range from Shelley's "To a Skylark" to the impassioned "Renascence" of Edna St. Vincent Millay and to Edward Lear's whimsical "The Owl and the Pussycat." 224pp. 5⅜ x 8½.

0-486-27165-X

COMPLETE SONNETS, William Shakespeare. Over 150 exquisite poems deal with love, friendship, the tyranny of time, beauty's evanescence, death and other themes in language of remarkable power, precision and beauty. Glossary of archaic terms. 80pp. 5³⁄₁₆ x 8¼.   0-486-26686-9

HISTORIC HOMES OF THE AMERICAN PRESIDENTS, Second, Revised Edition, Irvin Haas. A traveler's guide to American Presidential homes, most open to the public, depicting and describing homes occupied by every American President from George Washington to George Bush. With visiting hours, admission charges, travel routes. 175 photographs. Index. 160pp. 8¼ x 11.   0-486-26751-2

THE WIT AND HUMOR OF OSCAR WILDE, Alvin Redman (ed.). More than 1,000 ripostes, paradoxes, wisecracks: Work is the curse of the drinking classes; I can resist everything except temptation; etc. 258pp. 5⅜ x 8½.   0-486-20602-5

SHAKESPEARE LEXICON AND QUOTATION DICTIONARY, Alexander Schmidt. Full definitions, locations, shades of meaning in every word in plays and poems. More than 50,000 exact quotations. 1,485pp. 6½ x 9¼. 2-vol. set.
Vol. 1: 0-486-22726-X   Vol. 2: 0-486-22727-8

SELECTED POEMS, Emily Dickinson. Over 100 best-known, best-loved poems by one of America's foremost poets, reprinted from authoritative early editions. No comparable edition at this price. Index of first lines. 64pp. 5³⁄₁₆ x 8¼. 0-486-26466-1

THE INSIDIOUS DR. FU-MANCHU, Sax Rohmer. The first of the popular mystery series introduces a pair of English detectives to their archnemesis, the diabolical Dr. Fu-Manchu. Flavorful atmosphere, fast-paced action, and colorful characters enliven this classic of the genre. 208pp. 5³⁄₁₆ x 8¼.   0-486-29898-1

CATALOG OF DOVER BOOKS

LIGHT AND SHADE: A Classic Approach to Three-Dimensional Drawing, Mrs. Mary P. Merrifield. Handy reference clearly demonstrates principles of light and shade by revealing effects of common daylight, sunshine, and candle or artificial light on geometrical solids. 13 plates. 64pp. 5⅜ x 8½. 0-486-44143-1

ASTROLOGY AND ASTRONOMY: A Pictorial Archive of Signs and Symbols, Ernst and Johanna Lehner. Treasure trove of stories, lore, and myth, accompanied by more than 300 rare illustrations of planets, the Milky Way, signs of the zodiac, comets, meteors, and other astronomical phenomena. 192pp. 8⅜ x 11.
0-486-43981-X

JEWELRY MAKING: Techniques for Metal, Tim McCreight. Easy-to-follow instructions and carefully executed illustrations describe tools and techniques, use of gems and enamels, wire inlay, casting, and other topics. 72 line illustrations and diagrams. 176pp. 8¼ x 10⅞. 0-486-44043-5

MAKING BIRDHOUSES: Easy and Advanced Projects, Gladstone Califf. Easy-to-follow instructions include diagrams for everything from a one-room house for bluebirds to a forty-two-room structure for purple martins. 56 plates; 4 figures. 80pp. 8¾ x 6⅝. 0-486-44183-0

LITTLE BOOK OF LOG CABINS: How to Build and Furnish Them, William S. Wicks. Handy how-to manual, with instructions and illustrations for building cabins in the Adirondack style, fireplaces, stairways, furniture, beamed ceilings, and more. 102 line drawings. 96pp. 8¾ x 6⅝. 0-486-44259-4

THE SEASONS OF AMERICA PAST, Eric Sloane. From "sugaring time" and strawberry picking to Indian summer and fall harvest, a whole year's activities described in charming prose and enhanced with 79 of the author's own illustrations. 160pp. 8¼ x 11. 0-486-44220-9

THE METROPOLIS OF TOMORROW, Hugh Ferriss. Generous, prophetic vision of the metropolis of the future, as perceived in 1929. Powerful illustrations of towering structures, wide avenues, and rooftop parks—all features in many of today's modern cities. 59 illustrations. 144pp. 8¼ x 11. 0-486-43727-2

THE PATH TO ROME, Hilaire Belloc. This 1902 memoir abounds in lively vignettes from a vanished time, recounting a pilgrimage on foot across the Alps and Apennines in order to "see all Europe which the Christian Faith has saved." 77 of the author's original line drawings complement his sparkling prose. 272pp. 5⅜ x 8½.
0-486-44001-X

THE HISTORY OF RASSELAS: Prince of Abissinia, Samuel Johnson. Distinguished English writer attacks eighteenth-century optimism and man's unrealistic estimates of what life has to offer. 112pp. 5⅜ x 8½. 0-486-44094-X

A VOYAGE TO ARCTURUS, David Lindsay. A brilliant flight of pure fancy, where wild creatures crowd the fantastic landscape and demented torturers dominate victims with their bizarre mental powers. 272pp. 5⅜ x 8½. 0-486-44198-9

Paperbound unless otherwise indicated. Available at your book dealer, online at **www.doverpublications.com**, or by writing to Dept. GI, Dover Publications, Inc., 31 East 2nd Street, Mineola, NY 11501. For current price information or for free catalogs (please indicate field of interest), write to Dover Publications or log on to **www.doverpublications.com** and see every Dover book in print. Dover publishes more than 500 books each year on science, elementary and advanced mathematics, biology, music, art, literary history, social sciences, and other areas.